I0815220

The Art of Living Without Walls:

Co Published by:

Living Without Walls

Non Nobis Solum

'Not for us but for everyone'

Written By:
Anneke van Waesberghe

Foreword By:
Susan Rockefeller

The Art of Living Without Walls:
Haute Couture Architecture

ORO Editions
Publishers of Architecture, Art, and Design
Gordon Goff: Publisher

www.oroeditions.com
info@oroeditions.com

Foreword: Susan Rockefeller
Book Design: Yasser Rizky
Water Colors: Tatiana Efimova
Chief of Photography: Martin Puddy
Proofreader: Nigel Simmonds
Chief Editor: Travis Kliever
Managing Editor: Jake Anderson

First Edition

ISBN: 978-1-954081-62-8

Co Published by:
ORO Editions and Living Without Walls

ORO
EDITIONS

Living Without Walls
Non Nobis Solum
'Not for us but for everyone'

Color Separations and Printing: ORO Group Ltd.

ORO Editions makes a continuous effort to minimize the overall carbon footprint of its publications. As part of this goal, ORO Editions, in association with Global ReLeaf, arranges to plant trees to replace those used in the manufacturing of the paper produced for its books. Global ReLeaf is an international campaign run by American Forests, one of the world's oldest nonprofit conservation organizations. Global ReLeaf is American Forests' education and action program that helps individuals, organizations, agencies, and corporations improve the local and global environment by planting and caring for trees.

This book is made possible by:

THE BEIGE

With Contributions from: Shigeru Ban, Yuma Horikoshi, William McDonough, Cherie Nursalim, Robert Thurman

Nature Is The
Outdoor Waiting Room

An Introduction To The Escape Nomade Philosophy

"She was incomprehensible
for, in her, soul and spirit were one
- the beauty of her body
was the essence of her soul.
She was that unity sought for
by philosophers
through many centuries.
In this outdoor waiting room
of winds and stars
she had been sitting
for a hundred years,
at peace
in the contemplation
of herself."

F. Scott Fitzgerald

I want to thank all the teams who have been involved in the "making" of this book. First, it would not have been possible without the support of Ueli, my business partner. He took over the day-to-day operation of the company so that I could write my heart out. Then Travis helped me with the editing, and during my moments of despair, he would always be there and help me out to finalize the book until the end.

I also like to thank Bill Barnett for being such a visionary by inviting me to speak at the hospitality investment conference he organized in 2015 before the hospitality industry's tent trend was set. One special thanks to Tamotsu for his creative mind to implement the experiences and lifestyle I envisioned around life in a tent. Outstanding performance and assistance from the models who now have become part of the book. Thank you, Sunbrella team, for providing such classic solid outdoor fabrics, and Biasa Bali Fashion for providing the clothing for the models. Thank you to my sponsors and all those fantastic people who know who they are and helped me with during the time of COVID. And finally, a special thanks to Martin and Yasser, who dug in until the bitter end.

Haute Couture Architecture

Escape Nomade tented villa at the Sanctuary in Ubud, Bali.

Craftsman in Escape Nomade.

Upcycled fashion by Txell Miras.

Bridging the Gap Between Nature and Architecture

Escape Nomade tented villa at Kapuhala Resort, Koh Samui, Thailand.

Living suspension bridge from aerial roots of rubber fig trees in Meghalaya, Northeast India.

8
9

10
11

Table of Contents

Foreword 13

I. **Bridging the Gap** 17

II. **A Day in the Life of Escape Nomade Sanctuary** 31

III. **Living Without Walls** 57
- The Art of Life 60
- The Invisible World 65
  - ~ Moment of Awakening 65
- Living Fearlessly 73
  - ~ The Buddha's Royal Reason of Relativity, per Buddha, Einstein & Wittgenstein by Robert Thurman 79
- Rituals 80
- Intentions 82
- Designing Your Life with a Personal Journal 84
- The Simple yet Extravagant Life 92
  - ~ Make Tea Time a Ritual 93
  - ~ Recipes for the Simple yet Extravagant Life 99

IV. **Global Paradigm Shift** 109

V. **Simplicity for Hoteliers** 123
- From Old Luxury to the Luxury of Simplicity 124
- The New Paradigm Traveler 134
- Elegant Eco-Travelers 141
- Creating the Luxury of Simplicity in Hospitality 145
- The Beige - Angkor Wat, Cambodia 150
  170
- Aarunya Nature Resort - Kandy, Sri Lanka 177
- Kapuhala - Koh Samui, Thailand 188
- Raffles Grand Hotel d'Angkor - Siem Reap, Cambodia 190
- Selong Selo Luxury Residences - Lombok, Indonesia 192
- Keikoku Snow Tent - Tokyo, Japan 194
- Kura Kura "Island of Happiness" Bali, Indonesia 198
- Experiences 198
  - ~ Royal High Tea 205
  - ~ Spa by The River 210
  - ~ Dining With Intent 211
  - ~ Picnics at The Sanctuary

VI. **Haute Couture Architecture Inspirations** 215
- Art Nouveau 218
- Wabi-Sabi 234
- East Meets West in Design 241
  - ~ Contrast and Harmony, by Shigeru Ban 245
- Modern Architecture 248
- Earthworks Art 249
- Design for the Environment 253
- Biophilia 257
  - ~ Timeless Mindfulness, by William McDonough 262
- Tented Architecture for Global Nomads 266
  - ~ Balinese Vernacular Architecture 274

VII. **Haute Couture Architecture** 279

Foreword

Susan Rockefeller

March 17, 2020

> *"The more simple we are, the more complete we become."*
>
> Henry David Thoreau

We all romanticize the notion of a more pared-down, simpler life, not because we are nostalgic but because there is truth to it. With simplicity comes awareness. We learn more about our true selves. Through reflection and gratitude, we are able to embody not our public but our private face, the too-often hidden yet far more authentic one. And in so doing, our relationships become more meaningful because we can choose those people in our lives with whom we want to be and accept us for who we truly are.

One of the many benefits of simplicity is that it allows us to strip away the nonessential, focus our time and energy on the things that matter most, and pursue our interests. In Anneke van Waesberghe's case, that interest is the very notion of a simpler life. Grounding into the beauty of the body and the earth, Anneke is one of the most creative people I have ever met. Her latest output, *The Art of Living Without Walls: Haute Couture Architecture*, is the culmination of a life in service to the earth and regenerative materials, a love letter to sustainable living and community work.

Anneke has impressively created a community in Bali's uplands, aptly called The Sanctuary, that embodies artisan craftsmanship and inspiration. She designs and produces luxury, eco-friendly, semi-permanent tents for both private and commercial use through her unique company, Escape Nomade. It's eco-luxe at its best: in harmony with nature and environmentally sound. Anneke's tents' bioclimatic design ensure ultimate comfort and use sustainable materials and energy-efficient construction, leaving the land virtually untouched. Above the Ayung River, outside of Ubud, a peaceful center for traditional crafts and dance, terraced with rice paddies and dotted with Hindu temples and shrines, Anneke offers visitors a divine taste of her beautiful and serene escape. I applaud her values, motivation, and vision for sustainable beauty, a concept around which she was amazingly prescient! Anneke is actually doing it, living her environmental dream with beautiful, natural materials and fabrics. Not surprisingly, hers is a vibration that people hunger to replicate, wanting to empower themselves and manifest the spirit of "living without walls".

It's a longing that resonates with me personally. In 1982 I had a transformative life experience that motivated me to think deeply about what I actually needed to be happy in life. I discovered that having less stuff, fewer obligations, and making more time for the things I love – indeed the essential things – allowed me to live more fully in the moment. I lived with the Inuit, the indigenous Eskimos of Alaska, who lived and made use of everything they obtained from the land. They constructed traditional clothing that required highly developed skills passed down from generation to generation. They view the animal as a gift that can never be wasted, wearing seal skins to keep warm and eating its tough, protein-rich meat. I learned that we could live simply but thoroughly, eliminating the excess that has plagued us, and more importantly, our environmental ecosystem.

When I think of the Inuit, I reflect on the root word of human – *humus*, meaning ground and earth. In this context, the Inuit and other indigenous cultures are the closest to being truly human. There is beautiful synchronicity between their system of living and our planet. Their dependency on soil and sea health has cultivated a deep respect for the planet that has been passed on from generation to generation. Now, it's time for us to develop this same reverence. Once we do, we will truly feel the value of the ground and its soil beneath us. And it will give us the strength to incubate and achieve a vision that can preserve this earth.

Today I continue to strive to create more space in my life for the people I love, things I appreciate and opportunities I want to take. Heart-centered and soul inviting, I decluttered my home, my wardrobe, made time for my passions – art, photography, and film. I removed toxic interactions from my life and importantly gained control of my time. The health benefits are a bonus: by focusing on what's most important, stress levels and blood pressure lower, and the quality of our mental, emotional, and physical lives improves. People who live simply adopt self-care practices, observing what they put inside their bodies, enhancing their health. They care about themselves and the future enough so that they don't abuse either their bodies or planet earth in the process of living their lives.

What is so compelling about a life less complicated? It offers two of the most coveted gifts for all of us adventurers: freedom and the preciousness of time. Simplicity is rooted in the understanding that the more you own, the more responsibility you have. The constant need to keep up often leads to stress and anxiety. Simple living means you can carry your home on your back, like a snail or hermit crab. You can spend the night in the most amazing places, with the most awe-inspiring views. You can immerse yourself fully in your environment, to be closer to nature. I am confident it appeals to us all on some genetic level due to our ancestors' ancient experience living a nomadic way of life.

So, longing for the simpler way of life is a form of nostalgia for the way generations before us lived. It's no accident that nostalgia can manifest in feelings of loneliness, disconnection and emptiness and is a conduit for travel away from the deadening confines of time and space. A portmanteau attributed to Swiss medical student Johannes Hofer, nostalgia joins the Greek concept of *nóstos* (homecoming) with *álgos* (pain, ache). Hofer coined the term to describe the homesickness of Swiss mercenaries fighting in the foreign lowlands who experienced an intense longing for their beloved Alpine landscapes. Anneke, in her wisdom, tapped into this sense of desire.

I met Anneke when I was in my mid-twenties when we were both living in the East Village in New York City. Her apartment was filled with the most beautiful European and Asian designs. She had this incredible way of understanding, way ahead of time, some of the trends that have finally come into the public eye, such as Marie Kondo's *Tidying Up*. Anneke was able to take design and bring it down to the essence of beauty, streamlining it in a simply striking way. She manifested beauty in her apartment, her garden and in her fashion sensibility. At the time, she started her non-profit company, East Meets West, which set environmental design guidelines, emphasizing the importance of both people and the planet. Anneke shined a light on the philosophy and need to merge the divine principles of innovation in the West and the minimal sensibility of beauty from the East. Her approach is rooted in a philosophical understanding of the benefits of both form and function, and I was honored when she asked me to join as an advisor to the company.

But what I remember most is being struck by Anneke's beauty, design sensibility and intelligence. She epitomized aesthetic taste, and because she has always integrated an environmental spirit through design, she has always been on the cutting edge of a transformational movement. Ten years older than me, I learned from Anneke. Truly she was my design and taste mentor and helped me cultivate my own sense of beauty in my home. I remember clearly her personal fashion sense: muted linens, cashmere in beiges and whites. Anneke looked as though she was in spiritual practice within the context of fashion and design. As someone who had just come back from living with the Inuit and understanding the importance of sustainability, I was very interested in her thought process.

Anneke was well-traveled by the time I met her. She went around the globe seeking the best design principles, whether it was Morocco, Europe, Africa, or Asia, honing her skill to take some basic armature of structure and figure out the essence of beauty. I was thrilled when I had the chance to travel to India with her. We worked with the United Nations Environment Program (UNEP), exploring alternatives for the jute to be used in clothing and furniture, which would boost the economy in Bangladesh and India.

Starting in Delhi, we made our way through Agra and Jaipur. We explored teak factories with expert artisans and headed to Calcutta and Mumbai, which was called Bombay at the time. In Delhi, we met with the Jain sect's head guru (traditionally known as Jain Dharma). Anneke knew him through her work with Mikhail Gorbachev's Green Cross International, an organization with a mission to convene global spiritual leaders to tackle sustainability and the interrelated threats from nuclear arms, chemical weapons, unsustainable development and the man-induced decimation of the planet's ecology. For her contributions, Anneke herself was considered a spiritual leader. I felt so fortunate to be there with her.

Anneke also traveled with the utmost style! She had a suitcase with her linens. She had her white clothes and her hat. We collected silk fabrics, and when we were in India, I had bespoke clothes made. I learned to take the essence of my uniform – pencil pants and a suit jacket – and make copies of it with different fabrics that we hand-picked in Jaipur. It was a lesson in humility as one moment we were in luxurious hotels and the next on packed, working-class trains, where we had to hold on to our luggage for fear of theft.

At the time, Anneke was on a mission to figure out her next step with 'design thinking', the philosophy of designing a product to ensure sustainability throughout its lifecycle. That is, will it be made for obsolescence and end up in the dump or designed for disassembly? Today the circular economy is much more part of our lexicon, but at the time, Anneke was one of the pioneers of design thinking. She had a huge impact on me. I wondered: how do you design a life that allows for sophistication, innovation, and beauty? So, our travels together made me realize how design, spirituality, and the environment can come together in a very powerful way. The people in India lived in spirit and reincarnation. Something was gripping about the idea that one can live a life that's both environmental and spiritual. In a sense, they are one and the same because the interconnectedness and understanding of one's place in the world and our dependence on all things is the core of our existence. At this time, Anneke was in the process of her design thinking and moving towards her own personal articulation of this worldview.

Now we know that Anneke's passion, her spiritual calling, found its home in Bali amid the temples and the altars and sacredness, where she has fully evolved. It's there that she came up with the brilliance of l'Esprit de Nomade. Anneke asked herself, and in*The Art of Living Without Walls*, she urges us all to ask: "What are the things that people really need?"

The Art of Living Without Walls reflects how years of travel and paring down the essence of how you can live in relation to nature. Anneke imbues spirit into all of the objects that we love. Her practice is 'design as prayer', and it is transformative and illuminating for those who have had the privilege of experiencing it. Now *The Art of Living Without Walls* lets us all enter her world and dream with her in l'Esprit de Nomade.

Nomadic life has been consistent from time immemorial. We have all been nomads; it's in our DNA. Our modern life has disconnected us from our past. It's time to reconnect to our ancestors towards a simpler way of life, bringing us back into our connection to the earth. I personally am grateful for Anneke and this book, which gives us all the reminder and opportunity to return to the life of the nomad, living our life from the perspective of our heart with independence and freedom, opening our minds and manifesting greater freedom and focusing on what really counts.

I. Bridging the Gap

"Connecting the invisible to the visible world"

Living Without Walls

Living Outside the Box

Living With Intent

Living Without Walls is living outside the box in elegant simplicity, in harmony with nature, and with intention. Haute Couture Architecture is the medium I developed to manifest this idea in the world. This book is the story of how I discovered this way of living and design, and meant to be a helping hand to others who wish to do the same.

Twenty years ago, I left New York City in search of a quiet life in the jungles of Bali. In return I received a life of abundance and simple luxury, and a new outlook as a designer and person.

I learned to engage with an unseen reality by tuning in to Mother Nature and tuning out the materialistic world. I learned that each of us can design the life of our unspoken dreams and that together we can reimagine the Earth as the paradise it once was.

We are used to experiencing the world through a set of assumptions that have been handed to us by authorities and "conventional wisdom." This is the shared reality, the paradigm within which we live.

Humanity is on the verge of a paradigm shift that will take us away from exploiting each other and the planet. I created Haute Couture Architecture to contribute to that shift, by presenting a simple-yet-luxurious lifestyle that unveils the hidden secrets within nature.

This book is for social entrepreneurs and designers with a conscience, those fearless individuals who can be change-makers in history and have more power than any world leader. I want to empower them to bring services and goods that people can trust, food and clothes that do not compromise health, and to do away with the cheap products that we throw away onto disrespected dumps after short-term use.

We cannot find these solutions with our old ways of thinking, we need to bridge the gap between the world as it is now and the world as we want it to be.

- *We need to bridge the gap between the visible world of the senses and the invisible world of intuition.*
- *Between comfortable living and responsibility towards nature and fellow humans.*
- *Between extravagance and spending money on a higher purpose.*
- *Between VIP city loungers & VIP nature lovers.*
- *Between the fear of not having enough and the luxury of simplicity.*

Finally, I want to bridge the gaps between all of us. My work is an invitation for individuals from all walks of life to take a closer look at nature, at themselves and to prosper more than ever by doing so.

This book is for those who are ready to fight against the continuing onslaught of overconsumption and the attitude that nature is simply a resource to be exploited. We have forgotten that we are ourselves a part of Mother Nature. We need her to survive and thrive. We need her food, water, shelter, natural medicines and the rhythms of her constant cycles. Within her, we find a place to relax and enjoy our lives. She is still there to enjoy; we still have a chance to open our eyes and learn from nature's beauty. She teaches us that we don't need complex technologies to improve the quality of our lives; instead we need to look within ourselves and investigate how to do things more simply.

> *"Simplicity is the ultimate form of sophistication."*
>
> Leonardo Da Vinci

- *Not having to wear the latest fashion is a luxury.*
- *Being offline is a luxury.*
- *Going barefoot is a luxury.*
- *Not buying products wrapped in plastic is a luxury.*
- *Discovering we have more self power than we thought we had is a luxury.*
- *Knowing how to live in harmony with nature is a luxury.*
- *Not having to be successful is a luxury.*
- *Doing what we love to do is a luxury.*
- *To be positive is a luxury.*
- *Happiness is a luxury.*
- *To have no money but be happy and fearless is a luxury.*
- *To walk through an uncrowded airport is a luxury.*
- *Being happy watching the sunset is a luxury.*
- *Being the perfect imperfectionist is a luxury.*
- *Not being attached is a luxury.*
- *To have access to information is a luxury.*
- *Not having to have luxury ... is a luxury.*

“Luxury must be comfortable, otherwise it’s not luxury.”

Coco Chanel

- *Privacy is a luxury.*
- *Giving back is a luxury.*
- *Freedom and time are luxuries.*
- *Working from anywhere is a luxury.*
- *Breathing fresh air is a luxury.*
- *Not getting stuck in traffic is a luxury.*
- *Not having a tight schedule is a luxury.*
- *Being fearless is a luxury.*
- *Being close to nature is a luxury.*
- *Not being in crowded places is a luxury.*
- *Not having obligations is a luxury.*

As I learned to live without walls, I developed my design philosophy of Haute Couture Architecture to reflect a new "luxury of simplicity" that I had discovered, I didn't always understand the luxury of simplicity, however. I uncovered it over time through my travels, my work, and my search for a new way of life.

My own life story takes part within the story of humanity, the one we call history. But this is not 'his-story', it is 'her-story'.

I was born in Holland and went to work in the publishing industry in my early 20s. At the age of 32 I sold my publishing company, Editions International, to the multinational Reed Elsevier. I immediately went on to found East Meets West, a nonprofit organization. Its goal was to create awareness and promote cross-cultural differences and similarities between Japan and the West in architecture and design.

At that time, my ex-boss, Eli, said to me: "You' ll never make any profit with that." I responded that it was my dream to help people and create a better world, as I left with the bag of money I had from selling the business.

There were not many women in business then, and it was my dream to pay tribute to women's integrity and show them they didn't need to be or behave like men to enter the business world. I wanted to create a better world inside the business world. Starting a nonprofit was the beginning but not by any means an end. The organization was a platform to bring my message across, similar to what I am doing now.

The East Meets West foundation encouraged cross-cultural awareness, and put a time stamp on the state of design in the '80s when we published our findings in the book, *East Meets West: Archaeology of the Present*. It was a time when designers and architects, by nature, still expressed their cultural identity. Over time the integrity given by those cultural identities was lost, just as animal species have lost their natural habitats. We traded our integrity for materialism, we learned to value new cars more than human friendships, and the result has been massive over-consumption.

By the 1980s, problems with the acceptable ways of thinking and acting were becoming apparent, especially in design and architecture; while modernism had produced some amazing creations, it also conceived abominable creatures of disbelief that rattled people's understanding of what architecture was all about. Square building blocks became the norm worldwide. Simultaneously global culture became obsessed with having more than enough, just for the sake of having it.

This loss of integrity started in the Western world and has unfortunately crossed all borders. It has been adopted by every individual exposed to it and resulted in designers coming to prefer an international profile over their cultural heritage. They lose their identities by creating products alluring to the avant-garde. Instead of noticing the start of overconsumption, designers and consumers alike diverted to what was trendy. All of us played a complicit role. We all willingly participated. We didn't pay enough attention to the importance of what comes naturally to us, the resource of ultimate inspiration.

We are the thieves of our own greatness; we robbed ourselves of the beautiful thoughts we had when we were kids, when we dreamt of doing something extreme or different. Instead of living outside the box, we replaced our dreams with unimportant daily routines.

While running my nonprofit, I traveled the world and spent time with artists, designers, world leaders, scientists and spiritual thinkers. I was active in the International Global Forum, and through it I was lucky enough to meet intellectuals like Carl Sagan, adventurers like Thor Heyerdahl, and wandering monks like 'Guruji' Sushil Kumar. As I interacted and worked with these fascinating people, I was able to catch glimpses of an emerging way of thinking, which I later came to call the 'Paradigm Shift'. When Guruji told me to let him know when I was ready to become a priest, I knew I was on the right path and that I had the mind and strength to help bring the Paradigm Shift into the world. At the time, though, I kept this to myself and lived a subdued life. I never shared what Guruji had said, and what it meant to me, with anyone except my good friend Susan when she stayed with me at his ashram in New Delhi.

During that time, I also supported the International Green Cross, headed by Mikhail Gorbachev, and was a member of many other environmental organizations. I continued my quest and worked hard to find ways to follow my path. The rapidly disappearing rainforest was our most significant concern at that time, which led me to work on projects with the United Nations in India, participating in developing a wood substitute made from jute fiber and a natural composite. Now, thirty years later, sustainable composite floors are a reality. The floors of the tents that I design today use a local product from teak dust and recycled plastic.

By the early '90s, I was ready to promote positive change in the world more actively and created a universal Design for the Environment competition through the East Meets West organization. We wanted to inspire architects and designers to find solutions that were less harmful to the environment; as they select the primary materials of a product, they are fundamentally important in creating a more healthy future. Their research abilities and understanding of local market conditions are also indispensable for developing a successful, sustainable product strategy.

Unfortunately, the potential for environmentally responsible production remained untapped in the '90s. The systems we have today were not yet in place, and it seemed we kept bumping into the walls of an old way of thinking. Though there were already some sustainable resources available, they remained untouched. Even though I was working closely with the Environmental Protection Agency (who adopted our rules and regulations for sustainable design) and the Design Department of GE Plastics, the East Meets West organization had to postpone the Design for the Environment competition. It was premature to expect designers and architects to catch up with our ideas. At that time, they were still not conscious of the fact that they had the power to reduce many environmental problems through their own design and integrity. Even though I found an army of followers, the result was not enough for the global impact I had in mind.

It took a hundred thousand miles for me to touch base where I truly felt I belonged, Bali. When I was a kid, we had an Indonesian girl from West Papua in my class. I remember her sharing a slide showing an airplane's wings, with stark blue skies above and forested islands in the sea below. After so many years and thousands of miles north, east, south, and west, Bali mesmerized me and made me stay. I left behind the two-car garage, the congested roadways, the glass and steel offices, and I never looked back.

By 2004 I realized that I could have an even more significant impact as an entrepreneur, so I returned to the business world to start Escape Nomade. I set out to provide sustainable designs that made economic sense. I wanted to prove that each of us could help solve our pressing environmental problems through our life choices. I certainly didn't start the business because I saw a demand for it, but because I needed to share my vision of a sustainable life. As if by fate, Haute Couture Architecture revealed itself to me as the vehicle to express this vision.

> *"If you have built castles in the air, your work need not be lost; that is where they should be. Now put the foundations under them."*
>
> Henry David Thoreau

When we go through life with a positive attitude, everything else around us follows automatically, even if we don't realize it at the time. At heart, I am a non-conformist who wants to promote change through creativity and inventiveness. I strive to tune in emotionally to what is going on around me, to intuitively understand what others want and need so that I may give them support. I hope my outlook can inspire confidence, faith and hope for the people around me. I believe in possibilities, miracles, and grace, and I invite these into my life.

Will 2021 be remembered as the year we brought enlightenment and more human connections to our lives, or will it take a few more years?

I like to show that the tents I live in and design certainly don't have the arrogance of luxury palaces. Tents give you the self-consciousness of living in an exceptional habitat. It can make you feel as innocent as if living in a tiny house or hut.

My personal journey led me to the architecture of a sustainable lifestyle that carefully places humans within the sacred landscape, that opens portals to a new paradigm. Haute Couture Architecture celebrates our connection with and love for ourselves and nature.

As I complete this manuscript, I look back on the year 2020, at all the trials and life-changes we have gone through to survive in this extraordinary period. We are just barely beginning to peek at the new world that lies on the other side of this challenging time. Mother Nature has pushed us through the eye of the needle. It is time to reflect, reevaluate, open up to new possibilities and dream of the world we will create.

II

A Day in the Life of Escape Nomade Sanctuary

"Connecting to nature and to ourselves"

Living Without Walls

Living Outside the Box

Living With Intent

I perfect my designs and ideas at my tented Sanctuary in Ubud, Bali, my home for the last 20 years. The Sanctuary is flanked to the west by the beautiful Ayung River and on the east by a smaller offshoot where the main river used to run centuries ago. The Sanctuary is almost like an island, with a sacred landscape enveloped by temples in the north and south. It resonates with the gods and fires the soul with inspiration.

Every ridge in the landscape, every hill and bump or bulge, every mountain and stream, has an importance ingrained with ritual significance.

The haute couture architecture of The Sanctuary was conceived from the start to reflect this cosmic and geographical axis of the sacred, which keeps Bali and its people bound to the universe's energetic forces.

From the tents, I can look out across the river at terraced paddy fields where farmers plant rice by hand. Ducks flock to feed on insects and weeds, where children hunt dragonflies with long sticky rods and catch fish in the river. Men prepare their plumage for the ceremonial cockfight, while others continue plowing the land until just before sunset or climb coconut trees to take home their harvest of the day.

When a Balinese priest places his hands upon the earth, he does not feel sand and dirt. He senses life, the power and resonance of the planet energized by the prayers and cosmic notions of Balinese Hindu culture. This same earth, rich in red river clay, is fired into bricks and transformed into temples as an act of service and a gesture to the gods.

The island's ceremonial epicenter is in the great native gods: the sun, mountains and sea.

Even today, many Balinese believe their gods live upon the mountains and in rocks, trees, the wind, birds, streams and lakes. They believe, and I too have come to believe, that Bali literally belongs to the gods. All human beings are but transitory tenants, the gods the genuine landowners.

People feel blessed to be in this place and feel its positive energy, if only for just a moment in time. My guests who can consciously feel this energy leave the place inspired and with a new outlook on life. Those who are not connected feel something but can't put their finger on it. They leave it unattended even though, unconsciously, something has happened. It is guaranteed that this 'something' will come back, unexpectedly, at another stage in life as a forgotten memory.

A Day in the Life of Escape Nomade Sanctuary

6.30 In the Morning

Each morning I wake up in paradise to the rising sun's salute. Before opening my sleepy eyes, I do a few simple exercises to improve my eyesight and tighten my facial muscles to wake up my nervous system.

I let good feelings propel me to breathing exercises; eyes still closed in a meditative sleeping position. Harmony and peace with my environment keep my rituals sacred and ceremonial.

Once dawn has spread across the land, I've dressed for a bicycle ride through the rice fields. The sun rising from behind the holy Mount Agung gives a backdrop to the farmers already at work.

Balinese offerings of rice and flowers from the day before still lay on the road. The chickens picking at it flare up in front of my bicycle.

The village ladies sweep the street in front of their family compounds, fluffing up clouds of dust penetrated by sunlight, projecting light shadows onto my path.

It is still early, and the roads are still pristine, oxygen-filled pathways free of traffic. When I turn a corner, the light of the rising sun finds me again. I take a deep breath of happiness and keep going, past the decorated bamboo *penjor* poles that celebrate the latest community holiday. The sway of rice in the fields, rushing water through ancient *subak* irrigation channels, and ducks crowding recently harvested fields are all a part of the morning concert that touches my senses.

A few farmers are already working hard to get as much done as possible before the sun starts warming their skin. We greet each other in this morning, a spark of delight for all.

I try to help the duck herder lead his ducks to the rice field but at no avail as they will only follow his flag. The ducks cross the narrow path, swaying as if one leg is longer than the other.

The clouds around Mount Agung stretch out over the horizon, past a long row of other hazy volcanic peaks waking from their sleep. A flock of herons flies graciously over the shimmering landscape, searching for a nutritious paddy on which to land.

At the end of my ride, I plunge into the pool to cool off and continue my exercise. The water is misting into the air as it evaporates in the morning sun. Soft music plays in the background and I enjoy the time alone as farmers across the valley continue their daily chores.

Later on in the day, surrounded by ancient trees, I walk down to the Ayung River. I soak up the silence of the untouched jungle, filled with tropical plants and huge leaves the size of a human. Butterflies and dragonflies intermingle with holy trees and medicinal forest herbs in a symphony of elements. My dog follows me and chases coconuts floating in the rushing river. Both of us wade through the water until it gets too deep and then climb up into the jungle to continue our walk.

8 O'Clock

Collecting and harvesting fresh fruits for breakfast is part of the daily routine.

Passion grows wild with passion.

9 O'Clock

An unexpected rain shower catches us by surprise and to stay dry we hide under large jungle leaves waiting for it to stop. Precious moments being so close to Mother Nature's breath and inside her womb fill me with delight. The torrent slows to a drizzle for a few moments and we run up the long staircase to find refuge in my tented home above. Watching the rain unleashes a melancholic feeling, muffling all other sounds. My lovely staff brings hot tea while I watch nature unleash its theatre on the shimmering leaves. It is a feast for the soul and makes me want to sink deeper into the cushions.

10 O'Clock

As with many creatives, I spend a lot of time surrounded by nature. Each of the walls of my tents open up. No matter where I sit, stand or walk, I always have a full view of the landscape around me. I do most of my writing in a small cabin-like tent by the river where, during the monsoon rains, I can look out the window and see giant fallen trees and coconuts rushing by in the floodwaters. Being close to nature is a time-honored way to relax the mind, allowing one's primal genius to flow in peace.

I went for a picnic with a friend who has a zoo and the baby bear joined us.

Towering trees surround the property. My mother Didi stands there in awe.

Gede deep in meditation during a break.

Esprit, our Labrador/Balinese mix.

Walking down to the river with care anc attention.

Noon

In the late morning, our cook starts preparing lunch. It always makes me happy to see her appear with a beautiful presentation arranged in a stunning palette of colors inspired by the nature.

Ginger flowers to decorate and enhance the palette.

2 O'Clock

We can peek at nature's changes during the day and through the seasons from the open roof of the Atrium Tent. The side extension houses a spa, lounger and shower/dressing room. Over the pool hovers the swinging sofa, a perfect place from which to watch the rippling water and the rice fields across the valley.

3 O'Clock

Early afternoon is the perfect time to be outdoors with old friends. In the early days of The Sanctuary, back when I was perfecting my designs and the landscape was wild, save for a few small tents, I would host nature walks and simple teas while we shared life stories and philosophy. It gives me such a great joy to look back at those times and know that, through my tented designs, the same feeling of ease and wonder has been shared with others around the world.

Pointing out what he sees that I did not.

By planting a tree I thank Mother Nature for letting us use her space in which to create this amazing experience.

Pouring homemade Ayurvedic teas.

4 O'Clock

Tea Time

Tea time follows, with a wide variety of home-grown fresh teas and herbs.

A time to relax with friends, clients and guests. Here the team from *Vogue* piles into the swinging couch after a photoshoot.

6 O'Clock in the Evening

Cocktail Hour

Late afternoon arrives in concert with the golden hour of light when the sun begins setting over the rice fields. The paddies are framed with red flowers, cacao and banana trees. I enjoy a happy hour vodka and tonic with my neighbor in the spirit of spirits paying tribute to a healthy life. During this time I love listening to 1920s music and experiencing an era when we were individuals and not just consumers, living close to nature, blissfully ignorant to each other's beauty.

House cocktail: Baby Vodka with *celang* flower that changes color from blue to lavender when mixed with lemon.

Lime zest.

Blue Butterfly Pea flower ice cube.

The golden hour between 5 and 6pm,
when the world starts to wind down and the
crickets start to wake up.

7 O'Clock in the Evening

Dinner

From garden to kitchen to table. Kadek Masak prepared a wonderful meal from these freshly picked ingredients. Aubergine à la Kadek.

Cooking outdoors in the grounds.

Waiting for guests.

From seed to flower.

From flower to eggplant.

The vegetable and flower basket is brought from the garden to the kitchen to create small masterpieces.

8 O'Clock in the Evening

Later in the evening, the open-air bathtub is filled with water and Indian Ocean sea salt harvested on Bali's beaches. Hand-picked flowers and oils permeate the saltwater. Candles are lit and soft relaxing music plays in the background. The fragrances of the flowers and aromatic oils bring a feeling of happiness. The moon and the stars are above. The world is at peace, both inside and out.

Mesmerizing after sunset.

The ancient volcanic peaks and serpentine river serve as a backdrop to my terraced landscape here on the south side of heaven. My tents are draped in hand-sewn, custom fitted luxury fabrics and lay there peacefully to be lit by the moon.

The Sanctuary is embedded in Bali's lower hills, which lead to the volcanically active Mount Agung and a range of slumbering volcanos. Emerging from these heights are the open veins of ancient rivers, their abundant water-filled bellies buried in the earth's depths millions of years ago. The water of the Ayung River, this river of life, runs wild with memories and moonlight as it slithers through. Living Without Walls is a way to bring our own lives in tune with the timeless rhythms of nature. It pays tribute to Mother Nature and serves as a wake-up call to her fragility, a fragility created by human ignorance and personal gain. In doing so, we also bring respect for the Sacred Feminine back to our world. For most recorded history, women have been treated with suspicion, as property, expendable, and without the same rights as men.

The Bali landscape, recalling the dawn of its creation.

III.

Living Without Walls

"Live outside the box, and perceive the invisible"

Living Without Walls

Living Outside the Box

Living With Intent

"Woman is a misbegotten man and has a faulty and defective nature in comparison to his. Therefore, she is unsure of herself. What she cannot get, she 'seeks' to obtain through lying and diabolical deceptions. To put it briefly, one must be on one's guard with every woman, as if she were a poisonous snake and the horned devil. Thus in evil and perverse doings, women are cleverer, that is, slyer than man. Her feelings drive Woman toward every evil, just as reason impels man toward all good."

Albertus Magnus, 12th Century German Catholic Saint.

During the industrial revolution we went through a paradigm shift that made us realize that all humans were reduced to the status of consumers and workers. The entire natural world was transformed into a property, a resource to be extracted.

Living Without Walls is a way to bring our own lives in tune with the timeless rhythms of nature. It pays tribute to Mother Nature and serves as a wake-up call to her fragility, a fragility created by human ignorance and personal gain. In doing so, we also bring respect for the Sacred Feminine back to our world.

For most recorded history, women have been treated with suspicion, as property, expendable, and without the same rights as men. By labeling women as inferior and owned, we also devalued an entire half of our world experience. Feelings, emotion, intuition, reciprocity, and Mother Nature herself have all been marginalized. This way of male thinking reached its inevitable conclusion with the industrial age. At that time, we went through a paradigm shift that reduced all humans to the status of consumers and workers. The entire natural world was transformed into a property, a resource to be extracted.

We derided the invisible world of inner experience as 'female fantasy' and unreal. We taught our children that change only occurs through struggle and that our thoughts 'within' are in no way related to the world 'outside'. We crippled and suppressed Mother Nature as a disreputable woman ... and now, unless we restore respect for her, she will tame us in return.

We have forgotten who we were before the concept of idols damaged us. Trying to be something or someone else cannot last forever however. The truth eventually catches up and forces us to look in the mirror of reality. A changed world still remembers us and reminds us of who we were. Mother Nature doesn't abandon us; she automatically informs our senses of what direction we need to choose.

The Art of Life

I like to look to humanity's ancient wisdom and the perceptions we had before we decided to create our new world, apart from nature. With ancient wisdom in mind, we now must leave behind those dogmas and sets of rules that are no longer applicable. We must go forward with that longing for something new that comes from remembering who we were, with an urge to grow organically at our own pace, without being rushed by anyone or anything that tries to influence us in mysterious or hidden ways. This desire to grow is within us, just as it is within nature. Grass doesn't need to be told to grow; it grows naturally by itself, and so do we.

As a natural result of our desire to flourish, we can now (thankfully) see another paradigm shift taking place. Living with pure, cold reason devoid of any real purpose has become questionable.

Women have claimed the role of positive change-makers in society and in the business world. Because of this, our world is broadening, in both its seen and unseen aspects. That broadening will open up the minds of the men and women who have been exposed to the new awareness and our increased capabilities.

Nine centuries after the German saint's quote was written, I connected my own life to the safe haven of Mother Nature to create her-story.

As I grew and changed through my self-taught approach into the paradigm shift, I came to call my new outlook on life Living Without Walls.

Living Without Walls is a philosophy in action, an antidote to the speculative philosophers that have dominated us for years.

Nature doesn't need us; we need nature to breathe, feed and fancy.

It is beautiful to see men's newfound empathy towards humanity, decreased ego and less interest in power. It is lovely to witness this positive mutation, to live during this paradigm shift, to see it happen.

For many of us, the paradigm has already shifted:

We are now approaching life from 'what can you do for me' to 'what can I do for you'.

By loosening our grip on egotistical desires and preconceived ideas, we can enter into real experience and find the path towards filling our life with every abundance we could ever want.

This perception of the world requires us to make the invisible visible and the unseen seen. It reveals a powerful hidden world of intention, feeling and imagination that we can use to change ourselves and the entire planet.

"Do more than belong: participate.
Do more than care: help.
Do more than believe: practice.
Do more than be fair: be kind.
Do more than forgive: forget.
Do more than dream: work on it."

William Arthur Ward

Getting rid of shoes, getting rid of ego.

Naturally harvesting information and thinking creatively, manifesting dreams into reality while lingering under a tree for tea.

Reconnect to yourself and to the natural world. Pack up the best of the old like a treasured heirloom placed into suitcase that has withstood the test of time.

The Invisible World

A life of natural simplicity points to an undiscovered luxury that has always been there, even if it is often too close for the disgraced mind to see, feel and experience. Anyone can grasp what the world offers. You just have to know how to tap into it with your in-built antenna.

Our day-to-day minds, filled with thoughts, are just the tip of the iceberg that is our inner experience. Typically, they only relate to the material world and our perceptions of others as they relate to it. In my experience, these thoughts represent just 10% of the processes taking place inside our bodies. By noticing the unseen, the intangible, the total experience of our surroundings and ourselves, we can begin to bring the other 90% of the mind to our conscious awareness. After years of working with and being inspired by the unseen world, it is important for me to share these values and how I apply them in my designs and my personal life.

Moment of Awakening

To bridge our past with the future, we need a new vision to reconnect and ground ourselves. Here is how I found my new paradigm, how I consciously flipped that switch to leave the materialistic world behind twenty years ago when I moved to Bali.

That change happened when I consciously held the flower of a blossoming tree in my hand for a single moment. For the first time, and all at once, I smelled its fragrance with compassion, touched the flower and looked at the shapes, the grading of the colors, the waving movement of the stems, the different textures; I smelled and felt its sap seeping from the stem. With patience, I turned it around and around and experienced its stunning beauty consciously for the first time. Its grandeur became grander with every moment. Then I looked at the tree and thought about its ancestry and creation; that moment was a life-changer. After this awakening, I knew why simplicity is so challenging; it is so close that we just don't see it. When things are too close to us, after a while they wear out. It is that same closeness we have with an old but comfortable relationship. We need to wake up to it again and become aware of its beauty. This beauty was always unconsciously present, but this very special little moment gave me insight into the dormant capacity we have as humans.

That capacity is the 90% that is sleeping in every human being. This energy can be activated by anyone, in the same way I experienced it.

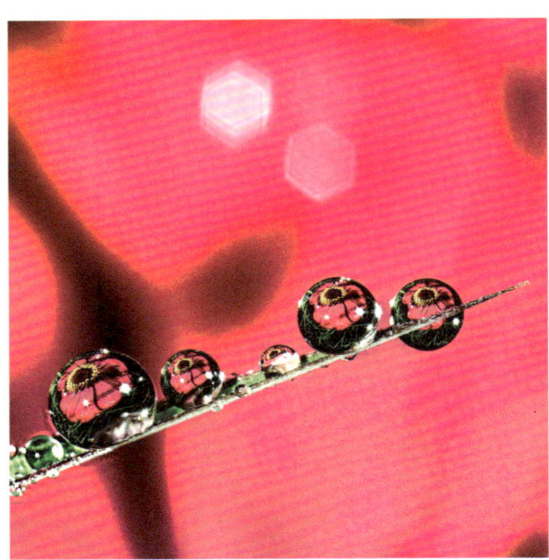

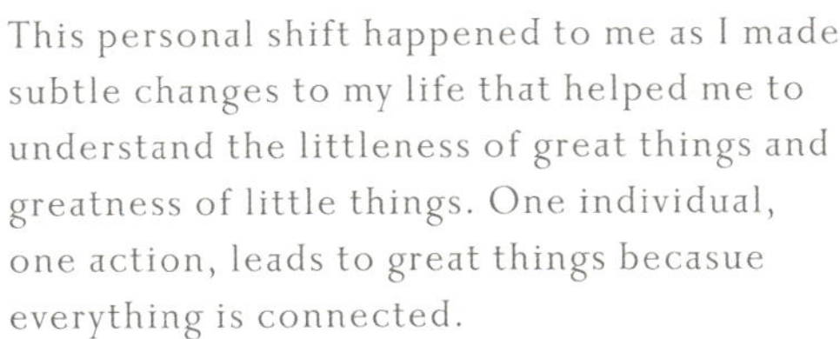

This personal shift happened to me as I made subtle changes to my life that helped me to understand the littleness of great things and greatness of little things. One individual, one action, leads to great things becasue everything is connected.

We never really see electrical power, only the results of it when it lights up a bulb or two. Before you've gone through a moment of enlightenment, you may become aware of a certain feeling that you can't quite identify. That feeling is like seeing the shape and form of an inner lightbulb that has just been turned on. Because you don't know and can't explain what caused it, you choose to ignore the feeling instead of dwelling on it and using it to your advantage. This is the critical moment to improve your life through an awareness of intuition, that sixth sense you were not aware of before.

You don't just see, hear, touch, smell and taste it, but you can feel that intuition deep within your guts. The inner voice that speaks to you isn't always taken seriously, but it is as real as your other five senses. Your intuition, the decisive factor, is an insight that can bring you to a higher level of consciousness. Only when you start trusting and believing yourself is it turned on, it is at those moments that your body is speaking to you.

That feeling you cannot identify is like seeing the shape and form of an inner lightbulb that has just been turned on, but the energy that created it you cannot see.

Your intuition, or sixth sense, sends signals to the heart, a part of your higher conscious self.

When you recognize that feeling, it is the moment to make decisions, trust it, and be truly yourself.

While speaking from the heart, you will be happy with the results because you can be certain that you did not lie to yourself.

Your decisions will always be woven like a golden thread throughout your life.

No matter where you are or what you do, whether you make simple material choices, or choices related to the heart, they will always come together and match.

When they match, your happiness factor will double and triple.

The world around us is an interaction between the observer and the observed. If there is no observer, there is no observation or universe as we see it. If we observe with limited capacity, we have limited access. The time has come to subscribe to the premium version of observation. The "for free" version of reality is not giving you the full picture. With the premium version, you can see both the visible and invisible worlds.

We place the filters of "life experience" and "expectancy" over what we perceive, and because of this, we often never really know or even wonder what others are seeing. Out of respect for those others, we don't need to force them to believe exactly as we do. Each individual has their belief system developed out of their experiences in this lifetime, just like we do.

When you are together with a friend, ask her what she sees in an object that you point out, and ask her to describe it in detail, what it feels like, what it represents.

From this explanation, you can understand the differences in your experience. You can understand and embrace those differences.

As you accept each other's differences, this act will bring harmony and peace to your friendship.

We need to forget our egos that conditioned us to the material world and rebuild our own identities in the natural world. Use that positivity as food for a new alter ego, constructed of the natural world's real experience. Our consciousness is in the creative mind; it is the mind that expresses our wishes, our desires, our aspirations and what we expect from life.

Our desires are fulfilled when we make those wishes reach our hearts. Do it with the attitude of knowing that everything will be alright, that you can live a conscious lifestyle with ease, that you won't be using up any more mental energy than you were before. Treat yourself as your own best friend to grow trust in yourself and in everything that you do.

The caterpillar radically transforms its body, eventually emerging as a butterfly. Today humanity is going through a similar metamorphic change.

Humanity is going through a metamorphosis, just like a larvae transforms into a fly, a tadpole into a frog and a caterpillar into a butterfly. One day, the caterpillar stops eating, hangs upside down from a twig or leaf and spins itself a silky cocoon or molds into a shiny chrysalis. A revolution and evolution takes place. There is chaos inside the cocoon and from that chaos comes clarity in a new shape. Within its protective casing, the caterpillar radically transforms its body, eventually emerging as a butterfly.

It is similar to what we humans are going through while moving into a new paradigm, a new era. We aren't shapeshifting, but we are changing the way we think about how we live, and we're accepting the limitations we need to face so as not to destroy our very nature. This transformation process is the process that will set you free and allow you to fly.

Our human metamorphosis also has the feeling of coming back to a home that we forgot about, after the things that happened in life took us far away from the source of who we are. A conscious lifestyle of living in the now will bring you back to the freedom you had before you got trapped in a world of others' desires and expectations. Like a free soldier after the war, walking home determined, even if it takes a month or a year of walking to reach the final destination.

The changes you make will often be ingrained with a hint of melancholy, as by realizing your dreams you are leaving behind is an old part of yourself. Just remember that you've traded them in so that you can fly out of your cocoon and emerge into a new world, ready to be filled with new desires.

At the height of the Japanese autumn, in one of Kyoto's gardens, a tea master asked his disciple to prepare for the tea ceremony. The disciple trimmed the hedges, raked the gravel, picked the dried leaves from the stones, and cleared the paths. The garden looked perfect: not even a blade of grass. The master inspected the garden quietly. When he finished watching, he silently shook a branch of the tree. He watched the autumn leaves slowly fall on the pristine path—the perfect imperfection, from simplicity to complexity to natural simplicity.

- Legendary story of Sen No Rikyu, master of the tea ceremony

Tanzan and Ekido were once traveling to get down a muddy road. Heavy rain was still falling. Coming around a bend, they met a lovely girl in a silk kimono and sash, unable to cross the intersection. "Come on, girl," said Tanzan at once. Lifting her in his arms, he carried her over the mud. Ekido did not speak again until that night when they reached the lodging temple. Then he no longer could restrain himself. "We don't go near females," he told Tanzan, "especially not young and lovely ones. It's dangerous. Why did you do that?" "I left the girl there," said Tanzan. "Are you still carrying her?"

- *The Muddy Road Parable*, traditional Zen Koan

> *“This is love: to fly toward a secret sky, to cause a hundred veils to fall each moment. First to let go of life. Finally, to take a step without feet.”*
>
> RUMI

There are many gateways to the invisible world of the sixth sense, but love in all forms is perhaps the greatest. I am not talking about simple romantic love, but the greater force behind it that is unattached and does not objectify. Quite simply, it is love for yourself and the natural environment around you.

It's only there for those who want to experience it. Only when you want it can it manifest. When you feel love, it is as if a sense of happiness surrounds you. It feels like you have discovered something new, a moment of nothingness that transformed into something.

When that feeling of love enters your hemispheres, you become consciously aware of what is natural and real around you; it is a transformative moment. Remember the flower story at the beginning of this chapter? You are now one with your environment and one with yourself in that environment. Your life may feel miserable, and then you fall in love, and from one moment to the other, you become the happiest person in the world.

Living in the now.

Fall in love every day, with yourself and with the world. What your heart knows is felt in your body. Unlearn that old belief that we cannot love ourselves. Only if you love yourself can you love others and know that it is not merely infatuation. When you live a life with less stress, that love can develop and find its way through you to others. It will simultaneously make you feel happier and healthier. If you do the work; if you love, are true to yourself and don't give up, you will succeed. When you trust yourself, you automatically live without fear and can do anything you want. That is the power of Living Without Walls.

Living Fearlessly

As I share my experiences with you, I hope you will find the inspiration to reach that same state of happiness that I have been lucky enough to discover. It starts with the simple understanding that you have unlimited possibilities that you can tap into, which will give you a happier and healthier life.

You are the creator and curator of your very own existence. You are the one creating your realities, positive or negative. Even if you aren't aware that you automatically influence the environment around you, you have probably noticed that your mood can make or break the day of the people surrounding you.

Often when people overreact or have bad intentions, these are derived from the negative experiences they've had in their lives. If you keep on holding on to the past and fail to create harmony and balance around you, you will experience a troubled life. Your environment will adapt itself to your negative thinking.

Every action generates a reaction. You are not only a pilot navigating the material and spiritual worlds, you are giving direction to both yourself and your environment. Both you and your environment consist of the same energy, as energy is all there is. Period. The energy just changes depending upon what you wish to do with it. You can leave it untouched, or you can discover that 'other' invisible world and have so much more world than you ever had before.

Depending on your mood, your environment will swing and go sweet or sour. You are the one giving direction to the energies that surround you. If you give love, you will receive love. If you help people, they will help you when you need it. If you lend money, you will get it back, though not necessarily in the same shape or form. It can take another shape at a time when you need it the most. If you are living with the faith that everything will be alright, that's what will happen.

BAMBOO STYLE

Living fearlessly without stress is the highest form of freedom that you can have. Live without the fear that you will not have enough love, money, or attention. In your mind, everything is abundant; you just have to attract it by asking with your heart, your soul, your commitment and your emotion. Once you visualize it, it will appear. You can live fearlessly if you trust yourself and trust that everything will be alright.

We live in a mental world composed of thought, feeling and emotion. If these three get together and merge, and we say the mountain will move, then yes, the mountain will move. Anything can manifest when asking our inner selves for permission to allow us to make the change.

We have to give our hearts the instructions for what we want to change.

Just say those instructions aloud, repeat them, desire your intentions deeply, and they will manifest at a moment in time when you are not even aware that they are coming true. The moment always comes in a hidden jacket, at a time when you expect it the least. As you develop your intuition, you will become aware of these moments and sense when they are happening.

Inspired by the stillness and harmony around me, I was able to move into a space deeply embedded in nature and live a peaceful life at the tented Sanctuary I created in Bali. This Sanctuary has become the provider of a sustainable lifestyle for myself and the people around me. I desired to live in peace and harmony with nature, and now I do.

Live without the fear that you will not have enough love, money or attention. Let go.

A friend said to me the other day: "If this is not Utopia, then what is?" It was all dreamed up by myself and created because that is what I quietly envisioned, and only shared with those who came to visit.

As I increased the power of my consciousness by opening up to intuition, I was able to manifest my intentions for life, the dreams I wanted to fulfill. Eventually, it led to an understanding of the power of this invisible energy itself. When you go into a state of intuitive awareness for the first time, you plug into a network that has always been there. Once you're plugged in, you discover many other gateways that lead there as well.

Living Without Walls creates a world without negative influencers. It is the art of living and curating life to your own liking. Stay away from negative news and people. Surround yourself with those you like, and live the life you want, the life you create for yourself.

"There is no separation or dualism between the physical and the metaphysical or between the material and the spiritual. Science gives us rational, logical, empirical, measurable and replicable tools and technologies which we need to function well in life. Spirituality gives us love, compassion, generosity and a sense of mutuality. We need these too."

Carl Edward Sagan

Success does not depend on the amount of money you have in the bank, but on your satisfaction, trust and faith that everything will be alright. There will always be enough when you need it. If you can truly believe that, it will happen, as this is how I experienced it. There was a time when I had little money, and it was a fun challenge to live on a low budget. I had a friend near me living in a monumental villa, but he had no money to spend either. Even when he only had five dollars in his pocket, he would feast me on the most delicious spaghetti aglio e olio. We had lots of laughs, and the bottle of vodka I brought usually did its job. We were happier than ever; we listened to music, watched the full moon and made jokes about things we'd experienced. I learned that by having a positive mind, the faith that everything would be alright and by not worrying about things, the payments would always and without fail arrive when I needed them.

It is essential to understand the difference between wealth and money. Do not let yourself trade wealth for money, nor wisdom for knowledge.

Read, gather knowledge, search online, listen to podcasts, watch interesting videos, meet and learn from interesting people.

All thoughts, both positive and negative, affect the development of our neurons and the synapses between them. This is referred to as neuroplasticity, the brain's ability to undergo biological changes due to psychological changes.

Happy, optimistic, and generally positive thoughts encourage the brain to produce serotonin, further enhancing those feelings. Serotonin helps us to feel less anxious, more calm and focused and generally stable emotionally.

According to Daniel Goleman in *Focus: The Hidden Driver of Excellence*, thinking positively will also enhance our creativity, increase our attention span and improve cognitive flexibility. Interestingly, it also helps widen our perception of self, making us more empathetic and concerned for others' needs.

As we think positively, we reinforce the neural pathways in our prefrontal cortex, the area that helps us to focus, control our emotions and be aware of our own thought processes.

However, when we are stressed, angry and anxious, we draw energy away from our prefrontal cortex. At these times, we are less focused, less creative, less alert to new input, have more difficulty controlling emotions and have difficulty working with others. Negative thoughts even affect our balance and coordination.

Our neurons connect us to the universe around us in the same way that the branches and roots of a tree connect it to that same universe.

The prefrontal cortex follows our intention in deciding how much to focus on a particular experience. If we focus on negativity, we will rewire our synapses and neurons to focus more on negativity in the future. Likewise, if we focus on positivity, we will wire our brains to be more conscious of it and encourage our brains to be more flexible in the future, further increasing our potential for happiness and positivity.

If you don't have the knowledge, you believe less.

Behavioral science has shown that optimists are generally more successful in life: healthier and more able to persevere through difficult times than pessimists. We don't have to believe in magic to understand that focused, positive intentions can dramatically improve our lives. Such attitudes literally change us physically, making us more aware of opportunities, more flexible and more able to take advantage of opportunities, making us more focused and determined on every level.

There is no separation or dualism between the physical and metaphysical – in between the material and the spirit.

> *"What quantum physics teaches us is that everything we thought was physical is not physical."*
>
> Bruce Lipton

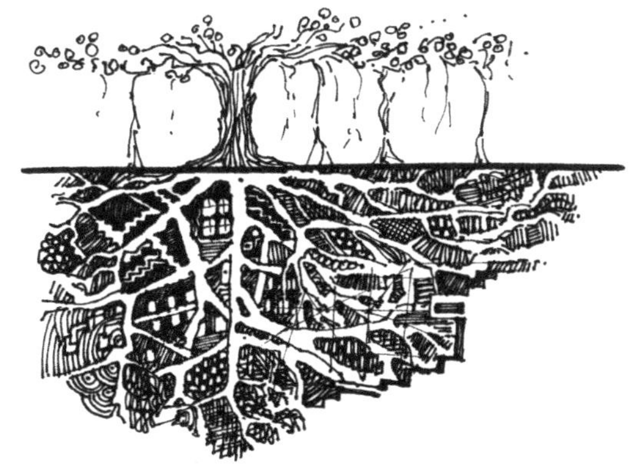

All that grows in the earth is connected and communicates through an underground mycelial network.

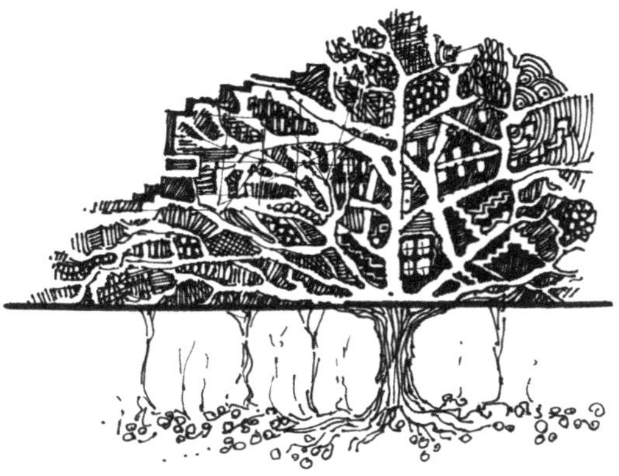

All life above the earth is connected and communicates through the air that we all breathe.

The Buddha's Royal Reason of Relativity, per Buddha, Einstein & Wittgenstein by Robert Thurman

"In 1926, quantum physicists discovered that there is no intrinsic reality to any particle. The act of observation itself influences the object that is being measured or observed. Since then, physicists have been going crazy trying to find something to hold onto. At the epistemological level there is no intrinsic objectivity.

Our unenlightened perceptual habit is to think that, "I am a thing in itself and that object is a thing in itself. I am my absolute, separate self, and that thing is its own inaccessible idea; pure form, pure essence, a pure indivisible particle."` That is our habit pattern. We've been used to thinking that when we see something, our perception is meeting a "massive facticity". We don't think of this as a described reality or a relational reality, we think it's an intrinsic reality.

We think, I'm absolutely me, and you're absolutely you. But when we say absolutely we actually use it lightly, like when we say, "do you want a little sugar in your tea?", and the answer is, "Absolutely!" But you couldn't put sugar in your tea "absolutely", because absolutely means non-relational, so the sugar would never reach your tea. We just say it for emphasis, but it fits with the way we interact with the world.

The bottom line is, since matter itself is void of being an intrinsically real, objective, identifiable thing, it's only relational and therefore completely inter-shapeable. The world is up for grabs, it's always being made and remade, so there's always hope to remake it better.

The word void is a relational word, it's a negation; something must be void of something else. When a person sees the objective non-existence of things, it puts a counterweight to their previous experiences of seeing things as existing in and of themselves. The existence and non-existence of a thing then press together, which makes it possible to find a truly relational way of dealing with the thing. You're completely interrelated with it. It's like being a tightrope walker; you're not in good shape if you're holding the pole straight up, you're very vulnerable to falling. So you take a big pole with weights on both ends, and that creates balance so that you can move relationally on the rope.

An individual is less than the infinity of all sentient beings on the infinity of worlds, but the infinity of all sentient beings is constituted of individuals. In some extraordinary experiences like being in love, or holding one's baby for the first time, human beings are capable of expanding their sense of identification. We have these little jolts of being temporarily relieved of our normal self-preoccupation, from the struggle with the vaster world that is unconquerable by us and can't be fended off by us.

If you attain nirvana you realize that you were always there. It's uncreated, unmade, beginningless. We're used to thinking of wisdom as the possession of a wise person, but transcendent wisdom goes beyond that person's possession. The person with transcendent wisdom gives their self to the universe. You become everything by transcending your habitually alienated self, by expanding beyond your skin, beyond the boundary between self and other. At such an occasion that wisdom automatically becomes naturally selfless and exquisitely skillful compassion, since you become fully empathetic. You could not bear that of course, if you did not simultaneously and inconceivably become the total bliss of wisdom, releasing itself into the pregnant void.

This is the meaning of the great Nāgārjuna's signal phrase: "Voidness the womb of compassion!" *(shūnyatā-kāruṇa-garbham)*. The void, in all its miraculous inconceivability, is thought of as a nurturing membrane, a vibrant cloth of that makes life possible. I thought of this master phrase recently as I listened to a wonderful physician lamenting the fact that 30% of babies in America nowadays are born by c-section, and thus miss the seeding of their billion fold gut-brain, their micro-biome, which comes from what he called "the anointing during their passage through the mother's birth canal"—their biological christening into life and health. Voidness the womb of compassion, doorway into the infinite lifestyle!"

Rituals

Before I visit my altar each morning, I read a little bit, even if it is just one chapter. It inspires me to make notes on my intentions. Once I have gone over these, I light the incense, feeling my intentions permeate the universe as I deeply inhale the sweet smell of frankincense. This ritual is an essential part of the day, giving me focus and providing the space for all I want to come true. It's a matter of visualizing what I want to manifest that day, accompanied by desire and deep emotion.

Our ancestors knew that rituals were a magnificent training ground for achieving a conscious presence. I use them as a portal to an awareness that I have the power to reach set goals.

Rituals slow the thought process and connect us to this moment, here and now. I am not talking about significant, ornate, cultural, or religious rituals. I am referring to simple daily actions that connect us to ourselves and to the present.

These kinds of rituals allow us to forget our identity and our worries. They help us to escape the crowded mind and move us into the present. That present may appear seemingly unimportant, but it allows us to enter a state of being beyond thinking, utterly focused on the act of what we are doing. It is similar to making love, reading a book, or painting; it allows us to go beyond our mundane conscious awareness.

A small bell gifted to me by a Balinese priest; a little statue given to me by my friend Susan; an incense and candle holder; crystals and stones. A small library of current readings and journal below the altar.

These rituals are tools used to get closer to the art of Living Without Walls. They give importance to the unimportant, the visible and invisible forms that we do not experience as we race through our lives, unaware of the essentials.

I have a personal altar that I created from items collected over time at different stages of my life. A small bell from a Balinese priest, a little statue given to me by my friend Susan, an incense and candleholder, an image of my mother, a carved sign I had made and an abundance of crystals and stones I bought at different times.

The night of each full moon, I fill a glass jar with water and leave it outside. The next day I wash my crystals and stones in the water, re-energizing them for the upcoming cycle. I then use this holy water daily to sprinkle onto the altar to honor the energies that empower me.

Rituals lead to a reflective state of being and help me to focus on becoming more conscious. While you concentrate on your inner self, try playing some healing music; sound energies are vibrations and they help in the process of feeling happier.

Intentions

I want to give you a way of creating your own utopia with your power of intention. We usually focus our intention on what others want us to be, on what a commercial society wants us to focus on. Move that attention to the world of nature; Mother Nature automatically informs our senses of what direction we need to choose. What you think shows what you want. If you don't know what you want, start to ask yourself questions, carefully. The answer is already intrinsically embedded in the questions you asked. You just need to keep formulating them until the question reveals itself.

Open yourself up and let your mind sink away into the natural world's clear yet invisible guidance. Give in, and you will see your path reflected in your thoughts and dreams. Then, use the tools provided in this chapter to turn your mindset towards realizing those dreams.

Implementing daily intentions led me to understand that if I can change, so can the world around me. Because I know that the invisible energy which surrounds me and is within me connects everything.

Designing Your Life with a Personal Journal

My personal journal is a powerful tool for opening up the invisible and creating the life that I dream, the life that I design for myself. Adapt the steps below to your own personal style and use this tool to manifest a utopia for yourself, just as I have.

- First, you need to figure out what you want to have or to change in life. Process it over time, visualize it and eventually you will realize it.
- It is your belief system that makes you who you are and determines what you can receive. If you worry about money, you will have financial trouble; if you believe and trust, you will always have enough to pay your bills. I have done it and it works! It's the power of reaping what you sow.
- What you think is who you are and what you will have, it's that simple. If you don't want to believe in it, that's your choice and your loss. If you decide to accept it, you will have health, wealth and happiness for the rest of your life.
- Finding out what you want is not always obvious, so you might have to think first and narrow down what you want.
- Next, deeply focus on those intentions. Feel the life you want to create and exist in, shut your eyes and breathe it in with your entire sense of self.
- Without focus, visualization and elevated emotion, nothing will happen. You cannot lie to your heart; it will know you are being deceptive it and it will not react.
- If you just say a wish, it doesn't work. If you want to be wealthy, for instance, you have to know what being wealthy looks like for you and visualize that as clearly as possible. Perceive the realistic amount you know that you can receive.
- At the same time, don't be afraid to visualize material things or finding romance; we all need those things.
- Imagine where the wealth will come from, what you will do with it, what your living situation looks like, where you are when you receive it and what the climate is like. Touch it, feel it, smell it; immerse the senses.
- Prepare a special journal just for your intentions. Focus on what you want for the next step in life and write down what you need to realize it. Ask for what you want, down to the smallest detail, and the answers will come to you automatically. Write them down, live them, and be convinced that they are what you want. You will start to realize that the answers were already embedded in the questions you so carefully formulated.

Prepare a special journal just for your intentions.

If you worry about money, you will have financial trouble; if you believe and trust you will have enough, you will always have enough.

The answers will come to you automatically as if you are harvesting them from the universe.

In the meantime, treat yourself to a picnic outdoors. It saves money and it's better than going to a restaurant.

- Read your intentions out loud before you go to sleep and again when you wake up. Through these acts, you send your intentions and wishes to the universe. If you do it with focused and profound feelings and emotions, the message will come across more clearly.
- The intention will filter into that 90% of your unexplored mental processes that lay beneath the surface. It is the part of the mind that notices and remembers information when you are not actively trying to tap into it. It will influence your behavior even though you do not realize it. Make it a habit for thirty days, and you will reap the benefits of making a wish come true sooner.
- The path generated by this intention will lead to questions and ideas that will ultimately lead to realizing your wishes.
- You have to do it religiously, so don't skip a day of focusing on it until it starts appearing.
- Write down your new findings, re-read the old ones every day, add more detail to your ideas and add new ideas and solutions as you progress. Your journal will be full before you know it.
- If there are things you want but find that the way to them is too hard for you, that simply means they are not part of your destination and you will have to change course.
- As you progress, deepen these intentions with an elevated emotion; add nuance by realizing what you don't want. I use the journal pages on the left side for this, ticking off the negative energies that I've left behind each morning to delve deeper into my positive wishes.
- As these intentions become more full and specific, start to analyze what you need to do to reach that goal and define and refine it down to the smallest detail.
- First, visualize what it looks like: the colors, the location, the smell, the sound. For instance, maybe you need a certain amount of money for a project; understand why you need it, then visualize the result of that project with all your senses.
- After that, write down the knowledge you need or the progress you need to reach to achieve the next step. Maybe you want to build a company, a house, an organic garden, or find the right person; investigate each step needed to actualize that intention in detail.

- Continue with the intention and read aloud to yourself what you still need to do to get there.

- To know the true meaning of your intention, go deeper into the meaning of the words you are using to formulate it. Repeat the process of studying what you need to do and slowly the results will start to manifest.

- As results begin to manifest, go deeper to get closer to what you want to reach. I have been following this daily routine for a long time, and it always provides me with results and solutions.

- Imagine that those things you want have already happened, even as you write and think about them. It just takes a little time for them to manifest in your new reality. It just is. It does not happen.

- When you re-read what you wrote down, you will be surprised to see all that has happened since. However, this change can only happen when you genuinely want it, feel it, visualize it ... and can almost touch it.

- Allow yourself to tune in to your frequency by drinking plenty of water, expressing gratitude, thinking positively, practicing acts of kindness and spending time with others who do so. Your energy levels will climb.

- Another way of reaching new levels is by moving your body through dance. Look around and notice the beauty; appreciate your surroundings. These are the vibes you want to feel: happiness, content ... and being on top of the world.

- Learn more about how essential oils can relax or invigorate you, or learn about the healing properties of crystals. Learn how to improve your life by deep breathing.

When I work with my journal, I feel like I am harvesting what I sowed, as if I have an antenna that makes things happen for me and my surroundings. Some people around you who are sensitive to this will be affected as well, as if your thoughts inspire them via osmosis. You will notice that those around you will suddenly take actions that lead to your vision; your life will change and your surroundings will become a better place for you.

The secret is that before this routine, you focused your energy on fighting the old instead of building the new. From now on, use that energy to build your new future.

The future is created by you and belongs to you because you have faith and believe in your dream's beauty, and that is what it takes to make it real. It is almost too simple to be, and it is that simplicity that will leave you and the people around you marveled.

Think positively, with a soft smile on your face and the faith that everything will be alright. The other option is to say, "I will never be successful". And in that case, you certainly will not.

Plenty of people stress themselves out by thinking they just need to work hard, but I effortlessly harvest my business ideas early in the morning when I am calm and meditative. I go through long stages when I don't wish for anything. During these times I catch up on my exercise and yoga, working deeply on my intentions and spending up to two hours a day reading and writing – leaving less time for other things.

The first time I noticed a result from following my intentions ritual was eight years ago when I realized that I needed a business partner.

I had been searching to understand why my previous business had succeeded and realized it was because I had a colleague who helped me close the publishing contracts. I am primarily a creative; I needed a business person to complement my skills.

My new business partner literally just walked into The Sanctuary one day. I didn't even realize that this was the result of my rituals. Now, after years of working together, he has become my alter ego and has made the company grow into what it is today.

The Simple yet Extravagant Life

Before I share new ideas with my clients, I use my sanctuary as a laboratory and proving ground for untested ideas. It is not just the sum of its buildings, but a complete experience.

While I am designing tents and the events that surround them I match the experience with the location. Every time I have a new idea I try it out. As I write, I am experimenting with permaculture, composting, organic gardening and new ways to present food at the table.

This work has led me to explore where my purchased ingredients come from, how they are transported, who made them and under what conditions and circumstances. Putting this knowledge into action creates a valuable worldview. If other people like the results of that worldview and repeat it, we can ensure the continued existence of earth and a human-friendly lifestyle for the future.

At The Sanctuary, we thrive on making the ordinary extravagant. It may sound like a contradiction, but we do this by living as simple as possible, close to nature and natural processes.

My foods are organic vegetables, salads, and fruits from my garden or our local market. The herbs in the organic garden are used for healing teas such as mint, hibiscus, rosella, tulsi, ginger or lemongrass.

Make Tea Time a Ritual

First, I boil water in my glass electric kettle. Watching water boil is fantastic; it is science and magic together. Witnessing the application of heat to still water and then the transition of water to steam is a great first step to the rest of the magic that happens as a result of this ritual.

I watch the water for the two minutes that it takes to boil. 'Crab eye' bubbles form, and the water begins to steam. Tiny bubbles dance and bounce and merge to form larger, hotter bubbles. Finally, steam blasts out of the kettle as the liquid turns to 'old man water', a genuinely roiling boil. And then 'ding', the bell goes off on the kettle and it shuts off automatically. Witnessing this sets the stage for making great tea.

Whether you have guests or are alone, you can prepare herbal Ayurvedic teas as I do, or whatever type of tea strikes your fancy. Spoon the freshly dried herbs and tea leaves into the teapot and pour in that gargling, boiling, steaming water, waiting patiently for the tea to infuse.

Take the cups and place them in front of your guests and, when the tea is ready, enjoy it slowly. With each sip, be conscious of the healing tea as it reaches the inner body and works its way through your system. The tea leaves its healing trace and pulls out toxins as it makes its way into and eventually out from your body. It's a meditation, as you are not focusing on yourself but on the ritual.

Reconnect with yourself and focus on the process of what you are doing. Get lost in that motion. By withdrawing the mind from automatic responses and turning to our six senses you reconnect to yourself. This experience gives you inner peace and makes you forget the noisy outside world.

My clothing is mostly white, so I don't need to waste time every day deciding what to wear. I feel free of sorrow as I have reduced my possessions to the minimum. Most of my material luxuries are now multifunctional and portable.

"By relying on female integrity, instead of stepping on Mother Nature, we give her relief by changing how we live from her and how we act upon her."

"Whether you have guests or are alone, you can prepare herbal Ayurvedic teas as I do, or whatever type of tea strikes your fancy. Spoon the fresh or dried herbs and tea leaves into the teapot and pour in that gargling, boiling, steaming water, waiting patiently for the tea to infuse."

The blue butterfly flower colors the tea into a beautiful aquamarine that delights surprised guests as they experience this for the first time.

From the Old World to Celebrating the New

Albee Tresna Kliever enjoys the moment.

From dominance to integrity.

From body and brain power to empathy.

From setting goals to making intentions.

From working hard to going with the flow.

From profit to progress.

From making money to having a purpose.

From 'how can I get this' to 'how can I help you'.

From materialism to living the dream.

From surrogate consumer to an extract of nature.

From ego to the essence.

From never having time to creating time for what counts.

From success to satisfaction.

From cheating to creating a good reputation.

From aggressive sales to empathy for the client.

From best product to proof of authenticity.

From destructive attitudes towards staff to understanding their situation.

From intrusive spying online to honest information.

From hacking to laissez faire.

From money first to actions based on honesty and trust.

From copying and making fast money to creating and enjoying the process.

From quantity to quality.

From worrying about reputation to being respected.

From robots to craftsmen.

Climbing towering coconut trees in the middle of rice paddies and sacred landscapes.

Recipes for the Simple yet Extravagant Life

Our homemade stove. We use the skin from coconuts for firewood, so nothing is left over.

Every Saturday we collect coconuts from the trees in our garden and make ingredients and supplies for the week. If we don't have enough coconuts, we buy them from a local store.

This process of making ten ingredients for health and wellness products out of ten coconuts is just one example of a sustainable way of living. Even if ycu don't have coconut trees or a garden, you can use a vertical hydroponic systems to fit in any size kitchen.

Coconut Oil From 10 Coconuts

First, open the coconuts and pour the coconut water into a jug.

Grind the coconut fiber, place it in a jug of coconut water and squeeze the liquid out of the grounds to create coconut milk. Set the fiber to these once all of the milk has been squeezed out.

Put the milk in a pot or kettle and boil on the stove. I like to add some turmeric for better taste and smell.

Wait until the oil surfaces to the top as little fisheyes.

Turn down the heat and slow cook for three hours.

Use a ladle or spoon to lift the oil from the surface, spooning it into a separate container.

Continue cooking at low heat. After one hour, spoon off the oil.

Usually we get about two liters of oil from 20 coconuts. Use the oil in your cooking, as a flavoring, for frying, or any other creative uses.

VOC Cold Pressed Virgin Coconut Oil

Obtain some old coconuts, grind the meat and squeeze out the milk as in the previous recipe.

Instead of boiling the milk, place it in a transparent bag. Tie the bag with a string and hang for 24 hours, after which the oil will have floated to the top.

Hold the bag over a container, pierce the top of the bag with a straw and carefully pour out the oil.

In addition to cooking, we use the cold-pressed oil as a massage oil by adding essential oils such as rosemary, mint and frangipani.

Body Cream

The same cold-pressed oil can be made into a body cream by mixing it with aloe vera and putting in the refrigerator. I use this cream every day after my morning rituals.
For a 100ml jar of body cream use:
Five Teaspoons of Coconut milk
50gr of fresh aloe vera gel
Two teaspoons of the cooking oil to soften the cream.

Young Coconut Yogurt

Buy a small container of organic, non-sugar yogurt for use as a starter. If you are vegetarian or vegan you can use apple cider vinegar instead.

Open three to four young coconuts, drain out the water and set aside in a container.

Scrape the soft white coconut meat out of the shells and place in a separate container.

Spoon the coconut meat into a blender, add some of the coconut water and blend until smooth. Add more coconut water if the mixture is still rough.

Sterilize a glass jar and pour the mixture into a jar. Add three tablespoons of yogurt or apple cider vinegar.

Either add a teaspoon of apple cider vinegar and consume immediately, or cover the jar with a cheese cloth and store at room temperature for 24 hours.

After this the yogurt is ready for consumption and can be stored in the refrigerator for up to one week.

Water from a young coconut is the perfect beverage for restoring hydration and replenishing electrolytes.

Coconut Soap

We make soap by burning coconut husks to ashes. To this we add coconut oil and pour the entire substance into a mould for a beautiful lifestyle product.

Soup, Flour, Coconut Chips

After making coconut oil, we usually have a lot of leftover liquid which can be used as stock for making soup. Leftover coconut fiber from the oil-making can be ground to flour and breadcrumbs for baking.

Old coconut meat can be thinly sliced and left in the sun for two days to dry. Then we roast it and add chili powder, salt, pepper and chopped lime leaves. We keep this in a jar and add it to our salads and muesli.

We use simple home-made natural cleaning products for maintenance. Baking soda and vinegar go a very long way and clean almost everything in any household. I even use it for tooth brushing and deodorant! We also make an effective and aromatic disinfectant by soaking betel leaves, squashing hyacinth leaves in water and adding rosemary extract or vitamin E oil to extend the expiration date.

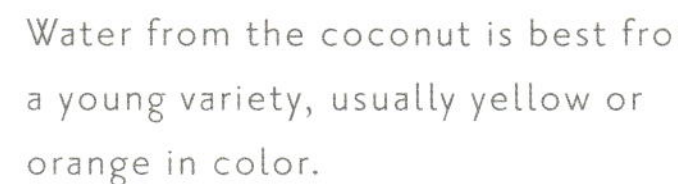

Water from the coconut is best from a young variety, usually yellow or orange in color.

Home-made coconut oil, body cream, water and yoghurt ... all made in three hours.

Oils, soap, flour and yogurt can all be made at home from the humble coconut.

Coconut Oil

Cooking and celebrating a picnic lunch together at The Sanctuary. We are all one family, from the staff that maintains our daily life to the architects and product development team that defines our future.

A new stage of my enlightenment came when I envisioned my first tents draped over a beautiful landscape in the small village of Semana, Bali. I was mentally ready to dive into a life of simplicity, to live satisfying my basic needs, and to let go of everything. This longing for simplicity, over time, led to a series of painless moments of growth. It started with the realization that I didn't want to be influenced by the outside world, I wasn't going to be worried about what people would think of me living in a tent. I wanted to challenge others to follow my example of simplicity and happiness.

Most people still see living in tents as a vacation or as an add-on to the garden, but why not vacation all year round? I live in tents and tents only, even the kitchen is a tent. Living in tents was the best decision I ever took, despite the rolling eyes of the people who did not think it was the thing to do. It was a major personal shift to ignore them, to be me, and to make it a personal goal to live a sustainable life.

When the invisible becomes visible.

A reflection of the light.

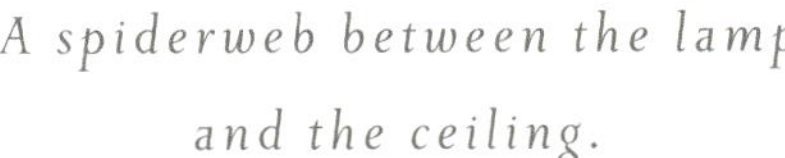

A spiderweb between the lamp and the ceiling.

The spiderweb is hiding until you see the light.

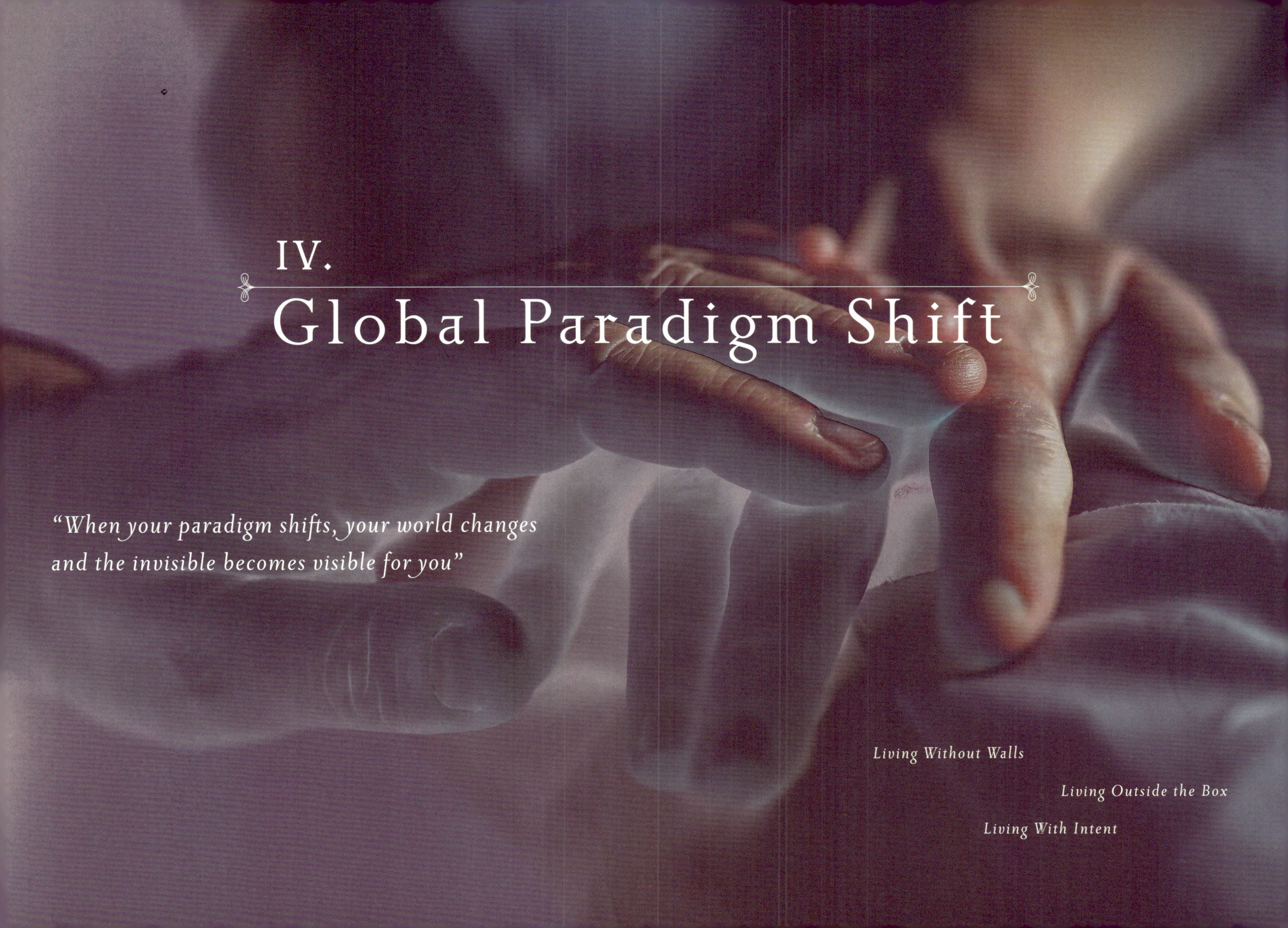

IV.

Global Paradigm Shift

"When your paradigm shifts, your world changes and the invisible becomes visible for you"

Living Without Walls

Living Outside the Box

Living With Intent

There is always light at the other side of the tunnel, no matter how dark it may seem.

We see humanity pondering adventures to Mars, but we still keep trashing our very own Mother Earth like a bunch of infidels. We seek another planet before we've even explored our own undiscovered natural powers and our own planet's greatness.

Society needs to change out of this old paradigm fast, but it will be a long process for those naysayers who claim to be rational while holding onto their destructive ways. They will fall into an empty hole, the hole that you and I have already filled with our wishes, our desires and a better life. Our paths will be easy and smooth as we don't fight and go with the universal flow.

I think of the process as going through the eye of a needle. This narrow opening is the perfect metaphor to clarify the longing for less that will enable us to enter new dimensions. These dimensions cannot be seen or experienced by those still focused on the material world.

"More the knowledge,
lesser the ego.
Lesser the knowledge,
more the ego."

Albert Einstein

Through the years, my personal paradigm shift led me away from the rat race of New York City to a luxuriously simple life in Bali. Similar shifts in consciousness are happening to millions worldwide as they wake up from the dream of materialism and into the real world of experience and intuition. Once we've gone through this needle's eye, we become more aware of and concerned for both nature and our other fellow humans. As more and more of us make the shift, a global paradigm shift starts to occur and becomes more visible to those on the verge.

A fundamental change happens when the puzzle doesn't fit anymore, and it seems the time has come.

As I write, we are living amid a global pandemic. Our oceans are full of trash and the fish are in danger. The atomic doomsday clock is just seconds to midnight, major corporations and throw-away manufacturers continue to rob the earth; the rich and poor are more divided than ever. Ethnic nationalism threatens the entire world order. These problems didn't start overnight; they have been coming for generations.

More of us are waking up to the fact that we need to change, so there is light at the end of the tunnel. That collective feeling of urgency is the global paradigm shift.

When there is a new insight, we cannot continue learning things the old way by cramming the memory with endlessly useless information. New insights bring new light, they open up more possibilities and abilities for us as human beings.

Paradigm shifts are powerful because our paradigms create the lens through which we see the world. It's like a light is lit and there is that 'aha!' moment of new insight, of seeing something different.

New insights bring new light; they open up more possibilities and abilities for us as human beings.

According to physicist and philosopher Thomas Kuhn, a scientific revolution occurs when scientists encounter abnormalities that cannot be explained by the universally accepted paradigm within which scientific progress is made. Paradigm shifts cause a fundamental change in a scientific discipline's basic concepts and our willingness to see, believe and practice what has recently been proven.

Kuhn used the duck-rabbit visual illusion to demonstrate how a paradigm shift can cause one to see the same image in an entirely different way.

This discrepancy is the basis of my understanding that we are all different – and the best thing we can do is to accept and respect that.

When I showed this image to my team, each person saw it differently. It clarified the idea that everybody sees things through a different perspective. Some saw the duck first, others the rabbit. It is similar to watching the clouds with a friend; one sees a monster in a passing cloud, the other sees an angel, while the clouds themselves quickly change into new and different shapes. It's difficult to explain to the other what you are seeing. This difference is the essence of why we should always have respect for what someone else believes, because we just see it differently.

It often takes society as a whole a lot longer to become conscious of a shift in paradigm. We don't want to spend the money and energy that change asks of us, so we keep on going and ignore it. However, the roadmap has changed, and the old ways of thinking only lead to blank walls.

When society doesn't try to overcome these roadblocks together, they manifest as a hardship.

Novel science has proven that we can change our conditioned brains once we realize that those old limiting beliefs are wired for mediocrity.

Neuroscience shows us that the brain is neuro-plastic, meaning any conditioning to the brain can always be changed or reversed. This knowledge used to be in the realm of spirituality, but now we understand it is merely applying science to the art of living well.

The key to breaking apart blocked neural patterns is to continuously create new pathways. When creating your intentions, you can do this by repeating the changes you want to make every day for at least 30 days.

Kuhn used the duck-rabbit optical illusion, made famous by Wittgenstein, to demonstrate how a paradigm shift can cause one to see the same information in an entirely different way.

There is plenty of proof that the world is going through a crisis because of our lack of empathy. Those still in the old paradigm behave as if they have selective mutism, not of speech, but of perception. Selective mutism is an anxiety disorder in which a person who is usually capable of speech cannot speak in specific situations or to particular people. This selective perception is the sly tendency not to notice, or quickly forget, things that cause emotional discomfort, especially when they give conflicting information that challenges prior beliefs.

The organism that is the earth, and all of us as living creatures on, has become very ill. Because it concerns our health, we are all distressed about COVID-19. But what about the health of the planet? The plastic virus has been raging and been left unattended for years. We are all infected by ignorance and we keep making and throwing away plastic until the planet, and us on it, will no longer be able to survive.

This example is not just a metaphor but a fact. The sickness of ignorance causes sickness in the body for both individuals and the planet. People know that smoking kills and continue anyway. We know what unhealthy foods do to us, yet many still consume them. Often people don't worry about their health until they're too sick to recover.

We need a cognitive vaccine to help the skeptics and depressed critics who insist on staying in the old paradigm to catch up. Our minds were equipped by evolution with an impulsion to create, transmit and defend beliefs useful to our progress and survival. With this in mind, it is the right time to use our capacities to the fullest and allow our sense of right and wrong, sick and healthy, to take hold in society. It concerns the preservation of our lives and that of the planet. Once we open up to the paradigm shift, it is our responsibility to keep others from getting infected by ignorance and tunnel vision.

By failing to change, we falsely think we haven't caused any trouble, even though the consequences of our inaction cause humiliation to other people; cause social rejection for others, give some a bad reputation and even cause death. Even though our actions have created so many problems, we refuse to drown ourselves and be humiliated by the tidal wave of environmental issues. These problems don't concern us, we think. These are someone else's problems, and if we do nothing, who is going to notice anyway?

We think: "It is not me who is mute; it is everybody else." If you don't have the knowledge you believe less. Aristotle famously wrote: "The more you know, the more you realize you don't know."

Change is a long process. Educational systems are based on the old paradigm that still rules society. Belief in the old paradigm still allows women to be raped, mistreated, threatened and humiliated daily around the world. Wars are still planned, trees are cut and mining still desecrates landscapes we otherwise could enjoy. It's a long list.

A few who dominate want to keep their privilege, not only over society but also over our world's destiny. They are making use of their position to keep their privilege while crippling the planet. In a recent interview, I heard one of these characters say:

"I am here to make money, I do not look at the social consequences of what I do."

This attitude will keep the old world from the change we deserve. We are told to hold on to the old paradigm and not to trust anybody, including ourselves. Don't let that old paradigm fool you; don't be like a crab holding on to a rock, refusing the power within you to move. If you hold on and don't flow, your energy will be lost as you use it up just to hold on. You will be whirled away by the mighty flooding river that crashes you onto the next rock. If you flow, you will calmly swim to the shore.

The way 90% of us still live, is just to get by, without waking up to our full capacity as human beings. And provokes us to anger and envy and cripples us with emotional weaknesses that keep us down and hold us back from a productive, happy and balanced life. I don't follow the media, and I try to ignore its misinformation even when reported via friends and family.

A high IQ (Intelligence Quotient) was the determining factor for human worth in the old paradigm. We did not realize that a high EQ (Emotional Intelligence Quotient) is just as relevant, if not more important. Highly intelligent people are often single-minded and obsessed with a non-social pursuit. A high EQ delivers to us the mature emotional skills required to understand better, to empathize and negotiate with other people. Without this emotional intelligence, success will fail us in our private lives and in our careers. A no-ego approach is necessary to reach unlimited access and can create a kind of wealth you never before imagined. It's often the high IQers that are holding on to old values. Their memories of what is 'supposed to be' cannot unleash the new as easily as the high EQer can.

Every day we eat, buy clothes and go about doing the things need to have a safe, healthy and peaceful life. But our ego wants more. The ego is the starter kit of inner pollution, and it always wants more. Our human desire is expanding in a world that cannot fulfill the wants of our material desires any longer. We are reaching 10 billion people on our planet and there is no place to go. The other planets don't have tea or ice cubes for your cocktail! So that's not an option unless Virgin Air has daily flights scheduled to Mars.

> “We cannot solve our problems with the same thinking we used when we created them.”
>
> ALBERT EINSTEIN

Our egos encompass all the powers that keep us apart from beauty.

No matter how hard you try to avoid it, the media still confronts us with bad news, prompts and provokes us to anger and envy and cripples us with emotional weaknesses that keep us down and hold us back from a productive, happy and balanced life.

I don’t follow the media, and I try to ignore its misinformation even when reported via friends and family. From experience, I learned that to have a balanced life I needed to turn off that switch, live fearlessly and not let negative influencers turn back on the disturbing channel labeled ‘the outside world’.

Our lives are disturbed by turbulent times and media interventions only set standards for what we should look like, how we should behave and where and how we should spend our money.

The media knows it can influence our thoughts and emotions to make us feel inferior by bringing bad news. It then produces a clever solution by advertising products that promise to soothe those emotions that it brings up. There is so much good news and progress in science that gets less attention because most people have been influenced to become addicted to bad news.

If one person can change, and millions of people collectively enact and persist in that same change, the world will surely change as well. It’s all about the tiny things that become big. We often don’t notice great change until we have already reached a tipping point.

We have to learn to empower ourselves with the intentions we want to materialize. The immense power of consciousness, willpower and courage is being recognized more and more in this fast-changing world.

At one time, most of my friends were still looking at life through the spectacle(s) of the old paradigm, and it was hard to discuss the changes that were happening. Over the last thirty years, the paradigm shift has become more apparent, and I have chosen to live a life informed by it. The combination of these two things has made those conversations much easier.

It's time for us to drop the old paradigm that tells us the world will change by struggle, combat and fighting. It's time to embrace the new paradigm that empowers everyone to be kind to themselves, the people around them and the environment. You are one of the eight billion individuals that have that power.

Don't think that the way back to a healthy world is only through scientific discoveries, protesting against government and corporations, or even laws promoting waste in packaging and manufacturing. All of these things will be part of the change, but the paradigm shift is also fundamentally about moving our perception beyond the material.

In the late '80s I had the honor of taking part in many insightful discussions about the paradigm shift that was just starting to crack through the modern world. For years, a small group of philosophers met in the early mornings at Jim Wall's Studio in Greenwich Village in New York City. We got together early in the morning, talked until we were hungry and proceeded to walk and talk through the village. We discussed all that the eye could see, what it could not see and why. We discussed the visible and invisible, and the limitations that we as humans had in our DNA. There was no talk yet that we could change our own DNA. At that time, we never would have guessed that we could learn how to open up and connect with our unconscious. And we never imagined that it would be neuroscience that would connect us to the invisible and change the world forever.

When we go through life with a positive attitude, everything else around us will follow. That's the way of the world.

In 2020, the current virus outbreak is starting to give us new answers and questions regarding how the world must continue to change.

Human civilization must discover that we have the power to create change together; each individual has magnetic power, whether negative or positive.

We need to follow our hearts and make the positive changes now, while we still can. If all of us eight billion people do the same, we will bring change more rapidly than what we were taught to believe is possible. It will spread from one part of the world to the other with lightning speed.

Individuals need to understand that the world needs them to make the change and not wait for society, religion, or governments to do something about it.

> *"Live your beliefs and you can turn the world around."*
>
> HENRY DAVID THOREAU

Think
POSITIVE
Feel
POSITIVE
Live
POSITIVE

New and old paradigm thinking. My glass is always full or half full.

As individuals, we create demand, and we have the power to pay for the things we want. We can bring about that change once we understand that we have power and use it for the good of the people and the world around us.

This process is all a part of the new paradigm; it is not about 'them', but 'us'. We are the change-makers. We have the power to buy or not to buy, to do or not to do.

The islands of plastic floating worldwide all started with a small piece thrown away by one person. With eight billion people doing the same collectively, these single actions can change the climate drastically. Now we realize that when we buy something wrapped in plastic, we leave a striking footprint that changes our world.

> *"Never doubt that a small group of thoughtful, committed citizens can change the world. Indeed, it is the only thing that ever has."*
>
> Margaret Mead

I once met a gardener burning leaves. I noticed plastic mixed in with the pile and told him that the fumes would be toxic. He said it was OK because the wind was going in the other direction. It should have been obvious, but I had to ask: "What happens if the neighbor does the same, and the wind blows back towards you?"

Another time I was in a store and, social warrior as always, I made sure no one near me put their groceries in a plastic bag. I asked my fellow shopper: "Do you really need that plastic bag for one can of Coca-Cola?" No, not really, he replied sheepishly. As if he was a mute sheep caught in a herd, he put back the bag. "If you throw away that piece of plastic, it will end up in the ocean, and the fish will eat it, and when you eat the fish, that plastic ends up in your body," I reminded him. He smiled and replied: "So I should not eat fish?" I just nodded yes and reminded him not to accept the plastic bag in the first place, folded up the plastic neatly and gave it back to the cashier. I was not afraid of being disliked, I cared more about the bigger picture than what he might think of me.

Plastic and pollution are already living inside our bodies, creating unknown diseases with unknown impacts. You might think, why don't governments do something about it? They don't because we are creating the demand and we are the ones who choose to use plastic in the first place. It's up to us to make those changes as individuals – and watch as society follows suit.

Through the incredible power of consciousness, both in the mind and in the heart, there are no limits to our individual powers. Align that consciousness with an honest view of the changing world that we live in. We can sense that the paradigm has shifted, but many of us are not doing anything different. We run around in circles, bewitched by the media and social influencers who continue to dance to the tune of the old paradigm.

> *"Be the change that you wish for the world."*
>
> Mahatma Gandhi

This change is already inherent in the DNA of new generations. Perhaps in the coming years we will discover that because coronavirus forced the world come to a standstill, people began to introspect, to discover themselves and re-discover what is important in life, rather than simply obsessing over work and money. One of the great payoffs of the paradigm shift is that we are discovering wealth and luxury in the world of tranquility.

Young people lack many of our old limiting beliefs and can't believe the world is this way. They are in turmoil and disbelief about us grown-ups. Usually, they don't have the power to create great change until a young kid – like Severn Suzuki in 1992 and Greta Thurnberg today – comes along and demands our attention.

Post-Millennials live in a culture of choice, self actualization and freedom of expression. Some are eclectic, creating their spirituality from elements of various religious or spiritual traditions, yoga, angels, Native American beliefs, or even secular myths like that of Harry Potter.

"Whatever we discover in the future, we will always have to change first as individuals, as each one of us embodies the change itself. We cannot shape the future if we don't shape up first."

Trust yourself, have faith in what you do. Learn to be calm by giving yourself time for daily introspection, reflection and meditation so that you can put forth your intentions with less negative influences from the outside. These simple actions can change the world through the incredible power of our collective consciousness.

There are no limits to your power when you align yourself with your own trustworthy view of the world. The passion you feel in your heart is your inborn natural talent to change yourself and change the world. It's the most powerful force on earth. When you change, the world changes with you.

Years ago, before I changed from my old paradigm, I wrongfully generalized about those around me and labeled them unprofessional, disloyal, untrustworthy or lacking commitment. I failed to see the many incredibly outstanding, kind-hearted, empathetic, selfless individuals through the appropriate lens. I changed the old paradigm and shifted. My life changed drastically from being focused on what others thought about me to how I cared for others in the larger picture: the environment and life on earth.

Silence your inner know-it-all voice, close your eyes, throw your hands up to the sky, open your heart to your passion and emotions, send your gratitude to the world and say thank you that you are happy and healthy and alive. Send out that message of love for life and you will unknowingly, as part of a collective consciousness, affect the rest of the world. Feel that peace and let your consciousness acknowledge your feelings and let out a deep sigh of relief. Every second that you do something positive re-writes our planet's future and delivers a new energetic blueprint.

"Let us remember: one book, one pen, one child, and one teacher can change the world."

Malala Yousafzi

Simplicity for Hoteliers

"Considering preservation, local communities and the planet first"

Living Without Walls

Living Outside the Box

Living With Intent

From Old Luxury to the Luxury of Simplicity

The first tents I designed were used as private high-end retreats. Eventually, the hospitality industry caught up and for the last ten years I have been designing tents for boutique hotel projects.

Our clients are an eclectic mix, and I feel lucky to be a part of their projects. They are influencers in the industry and not afraid to try something new. They are out of the box thinkers; living without walls and sharing the lifestyle with their guests.

I have gotten so used to this group of visionaries (as well as the community of artistic global nomads centered around Ubud) that sometimes I forget the 'Old Luxury' concept is still out there in the world. It is churning away like a noxious machine that spews out one unmemorable, alienating experience after another.

I was ungraciously pulled back into this world quite recently when I booked a five-star hotel in Jakarta. My first impression on arriving was that of a Communist apartment block in an offensive neighborhood.

This five-star settlement (built by a famous architect) was a grouping of prison-like structures that claimed luxury, surrounded by unloved trees dug into cement-covered holes within an atmosphere of overhanging smog. Their promise of being "close to the beach" was betrayed by roads and nondescript buildings that had been overlooked in the pictures I'd seen when making a reservation.

The sensation of alienation crept up on me; sad feelings of ugliness tempering the fantasy I'd had before I arrived. It started in the entrance lobby of this behemoth, designed to look down on anyone who entered it. Distant staff members greeted guests with fabricated smiles, their 'kindness' spewed from throne-like towered boxes set above us.

It seemed that most people who sat having tea in the lobby restaurant were blind to the surroundings outside of the building, as if this was normal. They were in awe of the pastries, the height of the towering ceilings, the spectacular lighting and the fake kindness of the hosts who seated them. I sat down and watched one of these groups, each individual on their best behavior, each of them in their 'I am unloved' act, impatiently waiting for the waiter to bring the lemon that he had forgotten to put on the tray. None of them was in conversation with each other.

Those nomophobics were only paying attention to their phones; obsessively checking for missed calls, emails real or imagined, corrupted by fake news. The most important thing many of us miss, especially in public spaces, is face-to-face interaction with our fellow humans. Maybe it's tepidophobia, the fear of a badly made cup of tea? Or just afraid of crossing the line and striking up a conversation?

As I took my sabbatical from running a company to write the essays in this book, the coronavirus broke out and the idea that the world would never be the same started to sink in. In a way, it could be a lucky strike. Bad attitudes might change; acts of greed, pollution, the spreading of fake news or a virus might become punishable offenses. Being dishonest or a materialist could one day become a part of the past. Egos might shrink as people showed more empathy toward each other. It could become a world where the new 'me' became 'we'.

What if the world could respond to climate change and environmental destruction with the sense of urgency we see applied to this virus? Climate change will be the next crisis, and we need to act before we are all standing with our feet in the water from rising sea levels. We cannot retreat into our five-star fortresses while others wither away from inhaling and digesting our man-made poisons.

As people change behavior, public spaces like hotel lobbies need to be adapted as well. Estrangement from society can be alleviated by creating spaces where people are not overwhelmed by belittling and imprisoning architecture. People want to change because they can feel that they are suffering, whether they understand it consciously or not.

As my first landlord in Bali always said: "If you are in harmony and balance with nature and your environment, your life will be in balance too."

"If you are in harmony and balance with nature and your environment, your life will be in balance too."

Pak Ketut

The Luxury of Simplicity really works for me.

The genesis of Escape Nomade was a dream of humans living with the rhythms of nature in timeless luxury, free to come and go into the modern world as they pleased from a lushly appointed tented refuge. To me, that freedom is the luxury of simplicity. We strive to promote a sustainable, human and nature-centric worldview within the hospitality industry.

You can find simplicity in both the visible and the invisible, the seen and unseen, tangible and intangible. Simplicity is finding clarity and meaning of the invisible through events we did not know were there before. Events that went unnoticed, hidden by emotions and invisible to the eyes closed to them.

The luxury of simplicity is as if we hold an empty glass that is suddenly filled by the discovery of new meaning. That which gives purpose adds definition and refinement to life; it is here wherein lies the values of simplicity. As if evoked by forgotten memories, we naturally recognize simplicity as fundamental to life's art.

As I opened myself up to the invisible, this ever-present simplicity, I became a new me. The old me thought that the old luxury was the ultimate. I did not know any better. The old me felt that I had to do big things, but now I do them in small portions. Because the details of simplicity have become more visible and valuable to me over time, the new me has discovered there is more to life and that there is more value in every small little step I take.

Today we are thankfully not alone in this quest. There is a whole world of artists, designers and architects who bring the paradigm shift to the world through their unique styles. With their sensitivity to beauty and change, these creatives have a different, more progressive worldview than many. They have quickly grasped the need for change and are transforming the world by using less harmful materials and considering the earth's fragility. We can now see glimpses of a new world peeking out through the smog, like a butterfly emerging from its cocoon. Design and architecture will never be the same again, but history will.

In the new paradigm, our status has changed from 'what I have' to 'who I am.'

The New Paradigm Traveler

Classic designs give us a timeless feeling and become part of us. They impart a feeling of stability and belonging. Good craftsmanship and durability allow generations to become familiar with an object and enjoy its beauty.

Trendy ideas, however, are less rooted, more erratic and are not as durable. Our tastes often change on a whim as we seek the next trend. This way of thinking however will soon be a part of the past.

The global paradigm shift is an ongoing process, taking place collectively as well as individually. Once we experience the shift, the world changes with us. The world has given the signs that things have to change. This process is happening while we sleep and while we are active during the day. As we shift to the new paradigm, we become the change agents. Society will follow what we do.

As more people shift their tastes from the plastic and the trendy towards more profound meaning, the travel market has followed. I have watched it play out over the last 20 years. In 2000, we saw a shift away from mass-market tourism to more independent-minded travelers. By 2010, as the paradigm shift continued, these independent travelers started searching for deeper meaning and became what I call ‘mind travelers’. Now in 2020, as more of them start to value experience over perceived luxury, we have the advent of the ‘new paradigm traveler’. Nobody knows what the future will bring, but as we look deeper into these changes we can read a story of increasing individuality, growing respect for the earth and deeper awareness of others.

2000

Frequent Travelers

2010

Mind Travelers

2020

New Paradigm Travelers

2030

?

From the material girl to the luxury of simplicity.

2000: Travelers change clothing more than one time a day and always dress for the occasion.

2010: Mind Travelers nurture sentimental bonds with people and the environment. They dress simply and elegantly.

2020: New Paradigm Travelers embrace empathy and understand life is not about the 'me' but the 'we'. They are attractive in the way they move around and dress discreetly.

From outer to inner.

2000: The Traveler secretly craves respect and privilege.

2010: The Mind Traveler discovers the path of the inner spirit, traveling to visit gurus and wellness centers.

2020: Because they can relate to the presence of the invisible, the New Paradigm Traveler leaps forward into the unknown. They know that what they cannot see radiates at different frequencies and comes to them because they are sensitive to it.

From the comfort zone to authenticity.

2000: Travelers want to stand out and be seen.

2010: Mind Travelers seek to blend in with their environment, to merge.

2020: New Paradigm Travelers only desire to be themselves. They are clear-minded and trust their gut feelings.

From standing out from the crowd to the pioneer spirit.

2000: Travelers enjoy a low key celebrity status.

2010: Mind Travelers are forever seeking The Great Escape and spare no money to have the best.

2020: The pioneer spirit of the New Paradigm Traveler forever pushes them to undertake expeditions into the unknown. Without fear, they embrace all of life's great adventures. They take an interest in anthropology and participate in archaeology.

From personal knowledge to global awareness.

2000: Travelers read books and visit museums. Travel is their quest for knowledge.

2010: The Mind Travelers enjoy life-changing experiences in countries around the world.

2020: New Paradigm Travelers immerse themselves deeply into nature and culture, visit unknown abandoned buildings, ruins and historical sites. They lend a hand to local communities because they realize that they are connected to them.

From connecting to self to connecting to all.

2000: Travelers long to be remembered by others.

2010: Mind Travelers visit places where they hope to find enlightenment through their travels.

2020: New Paradigm Travelers are not alienated but rather comforted by other cultures. They get close to them and make people they meet feel good about themselves, connecting to a world that was unknown before.

From good citizens
to philosophers.

2000: Travelers are creative and gentle in what they do and say.

2010: Mind Travelers are intellectuals who can see life more objectively than others.

2020: New Paradigm Travelers are philosophers who make other people understand what has changed in the world, within themselves, and why.

From dreamers
to magicians.

2000: Travelers dream of a life of luxury.

2010: Mind Travelers are romantics, always seeking what lies beyond the next horizon.

2020: New Paradigm Travelers are clear-minded, using travel to experience happiness, self-discovery and well-being. They work only when necessary.

From visitors
to global nomads.

2000: Travelers are elegant visitors.

2010: Mind Travelers are temporary nomads; they act it and promote it.

2020: New Paradigm Travelers have become global nomads, living a detached mobile and international lifestyle without the idea of territorial belonging. Rather than focus on money and possessions, they practice simplicity to support their frequent transits.

- *The New Paradigm Warrior has NO-EGO because they have no longing for power.*

- *The New Paradigm Advocate makes NO-JUDGEMENTS because they accept everybody as different.*

- *The New Paradigm Champion has NO-REGRETS because there are no expectations.*

- *The New Paradigm Executive has NO-SPOILAGE because they want to conserve.*

- *The New Paradigm Conqueror has NO-MESS UPS because their thoughts are simple.*

- *The New Paradigm Winner has NO-LOSS because they are not attached.*

- *The New Paradigm Musician is sympathetic to NO-NOISE.*

- *The New Paradigm Philosophers are NO-STRANGERS to themselves. They recognize the inner person and always find the answers from within.*

- *The New Paradigm Gods and Goddesses know that the world as re-created by man was not created for them. They live in the awareness that heaven was created on earth by the unseen spirit.*

Elegant Eco-Travelers

Over the past few years, so many beautiful, alternative ways of staying overnight have brought guests closer to the natural elements. Luxury tents are one way, but these creations also include treehouses, igloos and yurts, even underwater rooms suspended from floating rafts.

Most of these innovations come under the brand of ecotourism, which is intended to be a low-impact, small-scale alternative to commercial mass-tourism that exposes guests to fragile, pristine and relatively undisturbed natural areas.

Sometimes, though, we see this concept bleed back into mass tourism and we again run the risk of overrunning and trampling our fragile planet. Ecotourism needs to be taken up and led by only those who want to conserve and behave responsibly. Whenever possible, local tourism over international tourism should also be encouraged; people are naturally more concerned when the environment in their own country is at stake, and they will fight to protect what is theirs. Additionally, local tourism is often less reliant on air travel, significantly reducing the carbon footprint.

When we have to travel internationally, however, we need to be concerned with conserving the environment and improving local people's well-being. We must also consider whether or not the locals want us there. Even though tourism might be useful for a country's economy, we need to learn that sometimes our influence is not necessarily welcome. It might be hard to do, but we need to encourage informed travel that is respectful of local cultures and promotes the area's history as part of the trip.

As I live by the river, I hear rafters screaming their lungs out as they float through the valley, running amok when they get off the river and see them walking around half-naked as they wait for their tour bus. It is painful to hear the Balinese complain about them, to see how tourism can hurt this beautiful island's fragile nature and culture. This new noise only started a few years ago, and it is heartbreaking to realize there were millions of years of silence before tourism arrived. In the evening, I breathe in the calm air and apologize to nature.

Travel needs to return to its roots as an engine for personal growth and experience.

Even a hesitant traveler who knows nothing about the local history can be guided by their intuition to feel the energy of a place, to engage the mystical unknown and absorb an unseen reality. Intuition is a dynamic force that can be held onto and embraced by each human's imagination. Once we have a chance to get close to nature, this sense of belonging and reciprocity, this spirit of the place, will influence and reinforce our instincts. Intuition guided our ancestors thousands of years ago, and today it is awakening the media-born generation again to use their instinct and trust their gut feelings.

Small things can help a great deal in bringing the paradigm shift to hospitality. Simply telling tales and stories of the local culture and teaching guests something about social behavior in the country they are visiting can deepen their experience. On the macro-level, hotels should provide funds for ecological conservation that directly benefit the economic development and political empowerment of local communities; we need respect for different cultures and human rights to be a fundamental part of how we do business.

Teaching guests about social behavior in the country they are visiting can deepen their experience.

Since the 1980s, environmentalists have considered ecotourism a critical endeavor allowing future generations to experience destinations relatively untouched by human intervention. I was involved in these activities thirty five years ago and sometimes I feel that things haven't changed all that much, except of course that now everybody can travel and the population has doubled. We are still talking about the same things. As the world's state has become an emergency, the concepts of sustainable, ecologically beneficial and culturally respectful travel must become a priority. The same issues we had then have worsened today, and we cannot solve these problems with the same solutions we had at that time. Thirty five years ago, the scope would have been gentler, but as it has become an emergency, it is time to be clear about what needs to be done.

It's time we increased the conversation around our hospitality hosts who use chemicals in their perfect gardens, in groceries from their wholesalers and in cleaning their interiors. How deeply do we think about what is making the toiletries so perfumed, whether the pillows are infused with flame-retardant PBDEs, or if that Instagram-perfect pool is overloaded with chlorine? The hospitality industry could be exemplary by showing a new direction to travelers that turns away from the normalized abuse of nature's beauty.

Hotels have the power to demonstrate effective, sustainable management. The industry has to evolve the rating systems and celebrate those who strive to create a better world, have a purpose and participate in community activities. Those that greenwash with minimal environmental solutions need to be demoted.

Hotels have a responsibility to train local staff and to learn from them as well. For instance, the community's authentic people can teach us how to use their often forsaken traditional cooking methods, which we can present and use to educate our guests further. After all, it's the people who work at the hotel that make the place so welcoming.

Creating the Luxury of Simplicity in Hospitality

Small Is Beautiful

The smaller the project, the more that can be done to protect and promote the environment. Small resorts let travelers enjoy a more peaceful respite, as they look out at nature's endless beauty in peace and harmony without the interruption of built-up space.

We encourage our clients not to count keys but to count what is needed for guests to have a memorable experience. This act is the key to getting guests to talk about their visit and the lifelong memories the hotel has created for them.

As a contribution and act to protect the environment, Escape Nomade selects projects according to the size of the built-up space. We look for designs that allow 10-30% percent of the total land for our overnight tents, with another 20% for supporting buildings. Unbuilt areas ensure that at least half of the property is kept green. When the tent resort has reached the end of its life cycle, the minimal footprint will ensure that the land can quickly revert to its natural state.

Keep The Land Alive

We recommend our clients leave as much native flora as possible. It is nature's architecture and it should be part and parcel of the guest's experience. Additional plantings and seedlings should be added to the land, multiplying them over time to keep the environment alive and healthy. We also encourage organic gardens on site, using locally grown seeds.

Reduce Energy Use

Our tents are designed to preempt a dependence on excessive natural resources used by allowing developers to build quietly without disturbing the environment with drilling and machinery.

The tents are designed for natural climate control. We help our clients orient them in a north-south position to protect from the sun, and open the sides to promote cross-ventilation. This reduces the need for air conditioning at most hours of the day; however, when required, we incorporate air conditioning only within the four-poster beds, instead of throughout the entire room.

Hotels must reduce energy consumption with minimal interventions such as teaching staff to turn off taps while washing hands, turn off the lights when leaving a room and introducing 'the hour of the candle' as soon as the sun sets.

Water-saving systems and greywater recycling systems should be installed in kitchens and bathrooms.

Respect Staff & Community

Our clients do away with the plastic smile of the 'Old Luxury'. We work with owners who create comfortable working conditions, encourage authentic smiles and serve food made with love.

Developers must study how best to maximize social and economic benefits to the local community, cultural heritage and environment while minimizing their negative impact. This could include donating 10% of profits to build or sponsor a local school and inviting the community for social and cultural activities at the hotel.

Train staff from the local community and involve their families as well. All sides stand to gain from the cross-cultural communication that occurs when staff, community, hotel owners and guests are exposed to each other's world views.

Use local suppliers whenever possible; be a hero by keeping profits within the community.

Reduce Waste

Our hotel clients refuse plastic as much as possible. When it is impossible to refuse, they reuse and as a last resort, they recycle.

Introduce reusable amenities, provide a new toothbrush only when asked for.

Introduce refillable glass water bottles instead of plastic in areas without potable tap water. Reuse towels and laundry without a foamless detergent substitute.

Bring Guests Close To Nature & Culture

Experiences should be included in the room price and the hotel must guide the traveler through those experiences. Many visitors are city dwellers who are shy to get close to nature and the local community on their own.

Enacting these changes should not be seen as an inconvenience but as proof of character on the part of the hotel owner. That character creates respect and invaluable word-of-mouth marketing. Social media will prove the hotel's value as a global, national, or community leader. Travelers don't lie about their postings; they are increasingly educated and curate their trip before leaving.

To have an amazing experience is not about sleeping on a soft pillow or being out in the open but about savoring, observing, feeling, detecting and discovering the environment. Through our tent designs, we aim to enable those life-changing experiences amidst nature.

Our guests can look at the stars from the open-air pool or bathtub. When the panels are rolled up, they may step outside the tent from any space where traditional buildings would have an impenetrable wall.

The tents also serve to create a splendidly theatrical setting, with lustrous luncheons and evening banquets on special occasions. Dances and celebrations are easily organized in an atrium pool tent.

We provide the experience of stepping back to a time when nature was pristine, when the ancient trees and rocks were still undisturbed. On the most simple level, we provide people with a comfortable portal to step fearlessly barefoot onto the grass.

Our aesthetic is about exposing guests to a sustainable lifestyle by bringing them closer to nature in cozy comfort while also providing exciting new travel experiences. It's not only about making money, but caring about the individual traveler, the environment, and taking care of the local communities.

Winter & Summer Tents
In the Alps
In the Tropics
Climatized
hot and cold
Natural Hot and
Cool Air ventilated
Durable for
a lifetime
Sun protected
Grounded
Waterdrops
roll off the dirt
A variety of
safety measurements
Rain proof
Lock key wooden doors
Splash protected
Heavy weight
Secure on all levels
Mildew and virus
protected

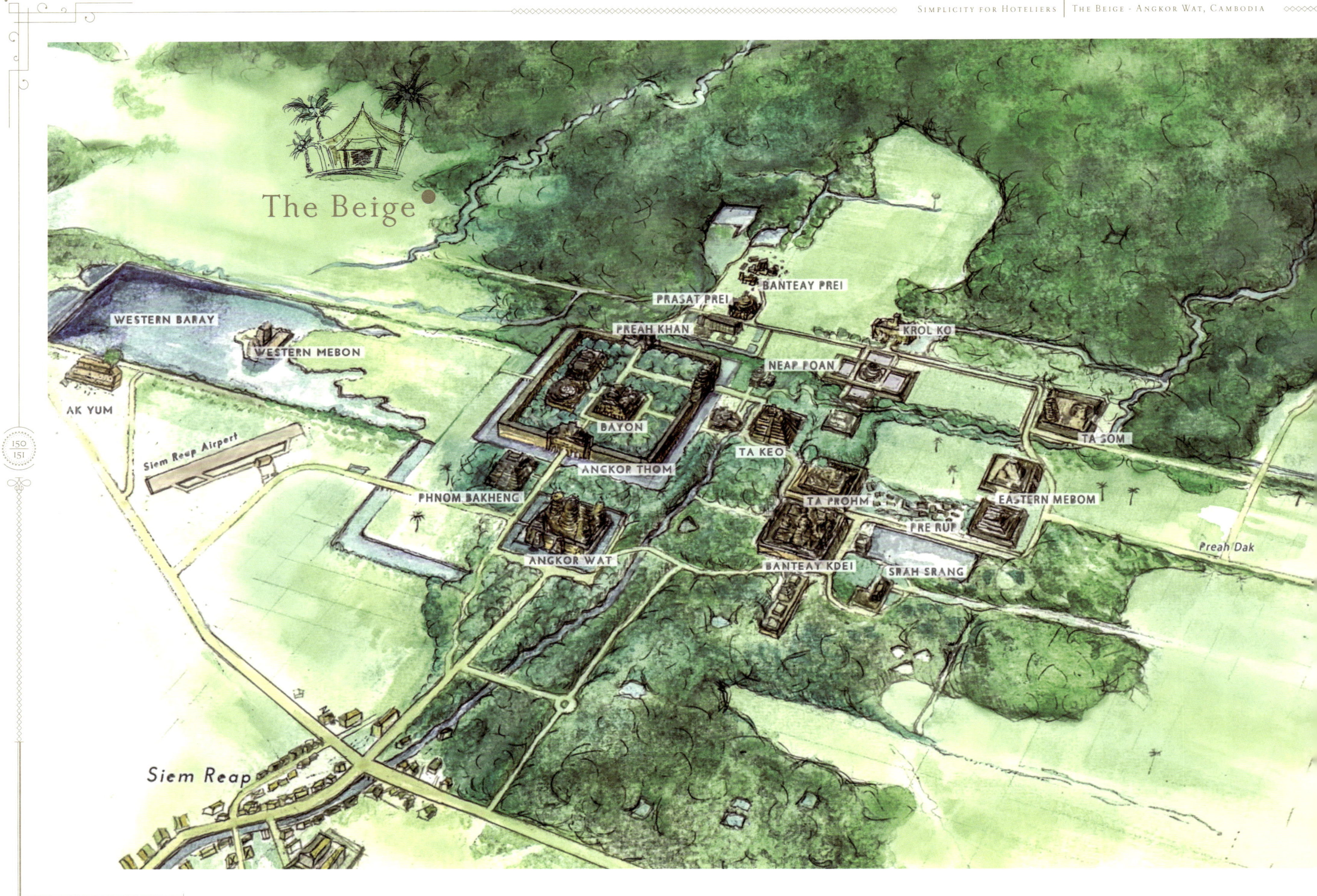

The Beige
WESTERN BARAY
WESTERN MEBON
AK YUM
Siem Reap Airport
PRASAT PREI
BANTEAY PREI
PREAH KHAN
KROL KO
NEAP POAN
BAYON
TA SOM
TA KEO
ANGKOR THOM
PHNOM BAKHENG
TA PROHM
EASTERN MEBOM
PRE RUP
ANGKOR WAT
BANTEAY KDEI
SRAH SRANG
Preah Dak
Siem Reap

The Beige
Angkor Wat, Cambodia

Mr. Tamotsu, the founder of The Beige, is a pioneering sustainability entrepreneur who dreamed of creating a magical place for real-world travelers. The dream has come true with his tented boutique hotel at Angkor Wat, Cambodia.

As the designer of his tents and experiences, I could feel that Mr. Tamotsu deeply understood the concept, and I gave him the support needed to implement the refined, detailed features that both of us admired so much.

アンコールワットに位置するブティックホテル「ザ・ベージュ」の日本人創業者であり、サステイナビリティに特化したビジネスのパイオニア、長谷川保氏。

彼は、彼自身の、そして世界を旅する人々の夢を叶える魔法の場所を創ることを実現しました。

テントの設計を行なっているプロが見ても、長谷川氏のコンセプトに対する深い理解と、細部まで洗練されたきめの細かい機能性を強く感じることができます。

The Beige has created an atmosphere that touches all six senses. All that the eyes can observe is a delight and merges with nature's sounds: the rain, the chirping birds, the whirling wind and the churning river. The sweet smell of flowers in the room invokes a deep breath with eyes closed. Food from the garden brings the taste and aroma of organically grown tomatoes, while hands rest on natural wood textures. The sixth sense, intuition, merges all of these sensations to guide us from the heart, mind and beyond.

The atmosphere at The Beige transports one back in space and time to a world of abundant nature, and it embodies the Escape Nomade principles of hospitality design. The ten hectares of the property is only 20% draped and dressed up with graceful tents; the rest of the sacred land is left in its natural state in the arms of Mother Nature, so that guests and staff may continue enjoying its pristine and waking beauty.

The tent interiors capture nature at its best, down to the soft alluring music we selected to play inside. Traditional Cambodian and Thai spas are available; there is also the option of a massage right in the room; the helpful staff will set it up especially for the occasion, to be sure guests have the best-extended views over the wilderness.

私たちの第6感に呼びかけるような雰囲気を醸し出し、自然の音と喜びを全身全霊で感じることのできる設計となっています。

雨、鳥のさえずり、吹き付ける風、川のせせらぎ、そして、柔らかく包み込む魅惑的な音楽。甘い花の香りに誘われて深呼吸をし、そっと目を閉じ、オーガニックトマトの味を楽しみつつも、手から伝わる天然木の質感。5感を通じて体や心に直接自然が語りかけ、第6感に届くような感覚は、日々の不健康な生活から解放されるようです。

長谷川氏のブティックホテル、The Beigeは、自然と人類が当たり前に共存していた時代へ連れ戻してくれるような雰囲気がエスケープノマドの持続可能性のセオリーに完全に一致しており、当著書の模範となっています。10ヘクタールの広大な土地は、わずか20%のみが優雅なテントとともに宿泊施設として使用され、残りはすべて母なる自然を手つかずのまま楽しめるまるで聖地のような場所となっています。

到着すると、スタッフの皆様が暖かく出迎えてくれ、テントまで案内してくれます。スタッフのサービスが隅々まで行き届いており、日中はスタッフがハンドメイドの美しい日傘をさして、強い日差しからゲストを守ってくれます。

Guests either go to the traditional Cambodian/Thai spa or enjoy a massage in these well-designed rooms, set up for the occasion to offer the best-extended views over the wilderness.

伝統的なカンボジアまたはタイマッサージに行けば、綺麗にデコレーションされたお部屋の窓から大自然が楽める、リラックスできるひと時が過ごせるお部屋に連れて行ってもらえます。

The open-sided rooms, flanked by the sights and sounds of the forest, can also offer a spirit of adventure as the resort's resident elephant, Rambai, passes by for a cuddle.

It was Rima, one of the co-founders of The Beige, who first discovered Rambai. During construction, Rima was living in a tent close to the elephant, then put to work by a group of Cambodian loggers. He spent months gaining its trust, and when the loggers moved on they they eventually agreed to let the elephant go. Rambai has since become the mascot of The Beige. Besides her regular diet, she gets fed by the guests with selected fruits.

テントのインテリアは、自然の最高の部分を切り取ったように美しく、音楽もこの上なく調和しており、魅力をより引き立てています。外観、内観ともに自然となじんでおり、リラックスして、健やかで安らかなひと時を過ごせるようになっています。

お部屋の中で自然の音や景色に魅了されている最中や、ブランコでくつろいでいる時に、お部屋の前を象や牛車が通り過ぎ、たちまちお部屋の中から冒険のような世界が広がることもあるでしょう。

象使いにサインを送れば、象のランバイを止めてくれて、触らせてくれます。ランバイはとても人懐っこい女の子です。直感に従い、怖がらずに彼女と触れ合ってみてください。

The resort also adopted a water buffalo family and a bullock, incorporating them into The Beige's daily activities.

The animals roam around a large watering hole, which is covered in beautiful pink hyacinth. Near the water, the tents glow in the soft sunlight. At night the firepit and candles are lit, offering a touch of magic when the silence of the jungle rules. While on the outdoor deck of my tent overlooking the lake that night, I discovered a million stars that set my heart on fire.

アフリカの大自然をテーマにした映画の世界に連れていかれるような感覚が湧くことでしょう。The Beigeの共同創設者のリンバが、象の近くのテントに住んでいた時、象のランバイは1ヶ月もしないうちにすっかりなついてしまい、管理人とも信頼を築いたことから、譲り受けてもらったのです。ランバイは今ではBeigeのマスコットキャラクターです。さらに彼女は、ゲストの皆様にお出ししているものと同じ、自家製の果物を食べて育っています。

After building the resort, the owners found an ancient Khmer temple on the land. Here, guests may enjoy a home-cooked vegetarian dinner prepared by an internationally trained local chef.

Mr. Tamotsu chose to honor the sacred venue by not touching the temple; it remains half-concealed and unexcavated. The floor is close to the ceiling but comfortable enough to enter this ancient and spiritual space.
To have world-class butler service in an authentic cave-like temple is simply magical and otherworldly.

アンコールワットの荘厳で伝統的なお寺を冒険を楽しめると同時に、オーナーが見つけたお寺が敷地内にもあります。

ミステリアスなお寺の探検の後は、地元アンコールワット出身の非常に腕のよいスタッフが作った家庭料理をご夕食にお楽しみいただけます。敷地内の庭園で育てられた、遺伝子組み換えなどをしていない自然のままのオーガニック野菜のベジタリアン、ビーガン料理がお楽しみいただきます。お寺は触らないことでその神聖さへの敬意を表します。発掘された時に比べてすでに半分の高さほどになってしまいました。床と天井の距離が近いですが、それでもゆっくりとと神聖さを感じていただけるには十分な高さとなっています。世界レベルのサービスをとても神聖な洞窟のようなお寺で体験でき、まるで楽園のような世界へと導いてくれます。

One afternoon when I was sitting near the temple at a picnic, an elephant and mahout from the village came by, hung around for a while and then went on their way. These authentic, unplanned, once-in-a-lifetime experiences are the things that I, and other lucky guests, will remember and treasure forever.

ある日の午後、お寺の近くでピクニックをしていると、象と象使いが私の目の前を通り過ぎてゆきました。どうやらお散歩中だったようです。手付かずの自然のなかで、様々な野生動物が混在する景色は、忘れることのできない一生の思い出となることでしょう。カンボジアの5つ星エコホテルの最高峰に君臨しているのも納得です。また、お部屋の宿泊人数の確認やロビーでのチェックインはなく、お部屋を借りたゲストの友人などとを集めてゆっくりと広大に広がる敷地で、誰にも邪魔されずに自然を楽しむこともできます。

ランバイの他にも、The Beigeの敷地内には水牛の家族と牡牛などがおり、様々な動物が地元の人と共存しています。動物たちは象と一緒にピンクのヒヤシンスで埋め尽くされた大きな水飲み場のあたりをよくお散歩しています。テントは柔らかな日差しで輝き、夕暮れまで自然光で明るく照らしてくれます。焚き火台とキャンドルに火がつけられると、ジャンルグルの静けさと壮大な自然のルールの魔法にかかったかのような感覚に陥ります。

As part of their efforts to develop meaningful community projects, The Beige provides both its staff and their family members with free education at a purpose-built school. They also fund local sporting events such as soccer and volleyball and started a local market so locals didn't have to travel all the way to Siem Reap. When I was there, I saw the strong relationships between The Beige management and the people in their communities; it felt like a large family where everybody cares. This family feeling was especially the case when the mother of Rima and Rado came for a visit. She lit up the hearts of everyone around and spread a sense of belonging and eternity. If there is sickness, they help each other; when there is a financial crisis, they offer food and immediate needs. At The Beige they provide staff family facilities, teach hygiene and also make guests understand that these families are happy with what they have and how they live as a result of their sense of community. In our isolation, we experience the same feelings as we strengthen our community spirit, neighborliness, food sharing and care, creating relationships of similar quality.

また、The Beigeはスタッフへの教育だけでなく、その家族までを含めたコミュニティープロジェクトを行なっています。中には地域に学校を作り地元の教育を支援するような外部コミュニティ活動もあります。私が滞在していた頃には、The Beigeのマネジメントとコミュニティはまるで大きな家族のようで、強いつながりを垣間見ることができました。リマとラドの母親がいるときは特にアットホームな雰囲気を感じられます。病気の時や経済的な苦境では食事を提供したりなど、お互いを助け合っています。スタッフとホテルの間でも、家族に対する施設を提供したり、衛生管理の講習を行ったりと、スタッフとその家族が充実した生活を送れるよう工夫がされており、コミュニティや近隣の強いつながりや、食事をシェアしたり、お互いの様子を確認している様子を強く感じ取ることができます。

また、交通手段としては、バイクやトゥクトゥク、ジープなど、快適な交通手段の中からお好みのものを選ぶことができます。

Unsurprisingly, The Beige has become one of the top five-star eco-hotels in Cambodia. There is no lobby check-in, just plenty of wide-open spaces where guests can enjoy the uninterrupted outdoors in comfort and privacy.

Today, nine months after my last visit to The Beige, many of us worldwide are experiencing the isolation of near-global lockdown and realize that we need to strengthen our own community spirit and neighborliness. Other forward-thinking hoteliers, and all of us as individuals, should learn from Mr. Tamotsu and share food, check on people nearby and create quality relationships.

象が食べているヒヤシンスの茎と同じ種類のもので、私たちが当著書の写真の撮影で訪れた際はスイのご両親がその茎で美味しいスープを作ってくれました。

彼らがいかに平和的に、心温まる日常を過ごしているかがうかがえる素敵な時間でした。人々の調和、違い、友情、文化の違いと共通点への尊重が感じられました。シンプルであることが財産となっており、西洋の価値観では貧しいで片付けられてしまいそうな状況とは裏腹に、家族のやコミュニティの絆や幸福に溢れる豊かな生活を垣間見れました。

私は、自家製で自然の掃除用品を使いメンテナスすることを推奨しています。

バリの聖地でも農薬や洗剤の代わりに重曹やお酢を使用していました。これらは非常に長い間にわたり実績があり、家じゅうのほとんどのものを綺麗にしてくれます。消毒にはピンロウの葉を使い、石鹸の代わりにヒヤシンスの葉を使用し、ビタミンEオイルとしてローズマリーを使用します。過去10年ほど私もこれらを使用していますが、環境にも優しく非常にお勧めです。私はArm&Hammerなどの、ごく一般的な重曹を歯磨き粉やデオドラントとして使用しています。感染症の予防としても効果があることも証明されています。*さらに環境に貢献できる魔法のような道具です。

The room amenities such as soaps and shampoos are made organically, as are the placemats, made from the dried stem of the water hyacinth.

シャンプーや石鹸などのお部屋のアメニティは、ヒヤシンスを乾燥させた茎を原料に地元で作られています。

Even grandma came out with her walking stick to see what was going on, helping her granddaughter Sui to grind the grain.
杖をついたおばあちゃんですら、何が起こっているのかをわざわざに見に来て、孫のスイの穀物を挽くのを手伝おうとしていました。

In front of the Presidential suite

Here Sui is at work at The Beige while her friend tends the garden. Many of the plants are sourced locally from the wild.

スイは友人が庭師として働く側、The Beigeで働いています。庭の景観は様々な選び抜かれた植物と、この場所にすでにある自然の植物が見事に融合しています。

Aarunya Nature Resort
Kandy, Sri Lanka

The Arunya is set amidst highland tea plantations in the Knuckles Mountain Range of Sri Lanka. The project is the brainchild of a father and son team: Dr. Lal Rankothge, a sustainable agriculture pioneer, and his son, Nath, the architect of these hybrid tent/villas. Lal and Nath chose not to dig new terraces out of the steep hills. Instead, they placed the tents high up in the treetops, sitting on tall modern platforms. I like to see my clients bring their own take on Haute Couture Architecture, in this case a tribute to Sri Lankan Tropical Minimalism, perched in the air like a bird's nest or the perfect hat that brings new life to a classic ensemble.

In Sanskrit, Arunya means 'first rays of the sun'. The decks and pools jutting out over misty mountain valleys amplify the subliminal, temporal experience of the rising sun, presenting it to the guests as their own special gateway into the world of the invisible. Yoga, meditation classes and therapeutic rituals soak this experience with the landscape into the body and mind. The Luxury of Simplicity is not just relaxation, it is transformation.

The Arunya has taken advantage of the fertile landscape by planting their own organic vegetables, spices and fruit gardens, used as raw materials for simple dining with family and friends in the arms of nature.

Constantly shifting views over the valley encourage a mood of reflection and contemplation. Organic vegetables, fruits and spices from the on-site garden add to the magic of simple dining experiences in front of the tents.

Spending time with the invisible reality that appears when we relax.

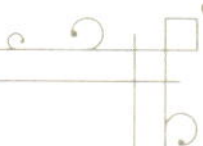

Kapuhala
Koh Samui, Thailand

Kapuhala means 'hidden tree' in Hawaiian, chosen here to signify the owner's goal of unlocking the hidden potential within their guests. This project takes the Luxury of Simplicity concept to active high achievers, with daily yoga sessions, a fully equipped fitness studio, 25-meter pool and even specialized equipment for triathlon training. While Living Without Walls can be about enjoying a simple cup of tea in nature, it can also be about sculpting the body and mind with the power of intention.

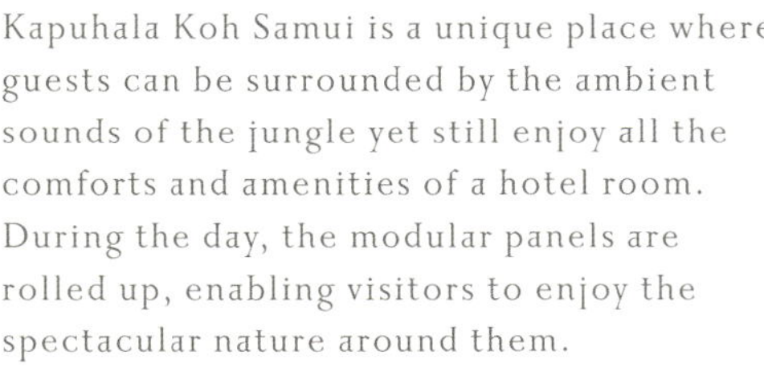

Kapuhala Koh Samui is a unique place where guests can be surrounded by the ambient sounds of the jungle yet still enjoy all the comforts and amenities of a hotel room. During the day, the modular panels are rolled up, enabling visitors to enjoy the spectacular nature around them.

Tented resorts like this offer a different way of living, out of the ordinary, a different perspective. Guests are invited to connect with the natural world and experience something as simple as waking up or taking a shower in an entirely new way.

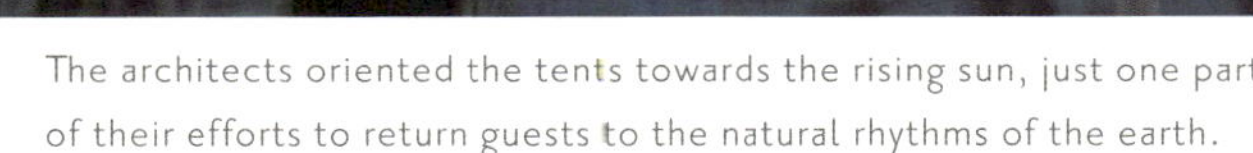

The architects oriented the tents towards the rising sun, just one part of their efforts to return guests to the natural rhythms of the earth.

Living healthy doesn't have to mean forsaking the little pleasures like cocktails at sunset. At Kapuhala, they're positively brimming with fresh herbs and unique infusions.

CAMUS
XO
MIDORI
KAPUHALA
KOH SAMUI

Farm to table dining is a safe and secure way of knowing that vegetables and fruits are organic and not sprayed with chemicals. No surprise the concept is popular; us humans we want to live a long and healthy life.

Gregory Hill, the executive chef at Kapuhala, believes as I do that dining should be both restorative and celebratory. Chef Gregory is passionate about changing people's perception of vegan food by applying plant-based recipes to fine dining.

All Day
Sombrero 425-

Wide views are exhilarating. When we step out into them we share our natural feelings of happiness with our environment; nature in return automatically charges our internal batteries with energy.

Raffles Grand Hotel d'Angkor Siem Reap, Cambodia

Raffles Siam Reap is located in a French colonial heritage building that has been lovingly restored and maintained. However, the old building was unable to accommodate crowds for conferences, weddings and traditional dance performances, so the owners came to us looking to create a new 250-person venue that would reflect the diverse Khmer and French heritage of the hotel. The space was a tricky one to fill, as it would require multiple tents and needed to be built around a historic wall that was salvaged from ancient Khmer rocks found on the site.

My original design was created to reflect the grandeur of the old hotel building and the precise symmetry of the nearby Angkor temple complex. In the end, the owners chose to reduce the space, nestling the building in between a grove of trees. My original intentions still came off in the interior space: a luscious hall draped in crisp fabrics, well lit by glass-louvered doors. It gives off the sense of ancient royalty setting up camp to entertain worldly nobles.

Selong Selo Luxury Residences Lombok, Indonesia

Our clients at Selong Selo have a spacious setting overlooking the wide curve of the beach at Selong Belanak. Rugged hills dot the landscape around, while bright sunny days are cooled by the fresh ocean breeze.

Selong Selo incorporates luxury tented villas set into the hillside, each with views overlooking green farmland and out to the turquoise waters of Selong Belanak Beach. The resort has been planned and landscaped to ensure every villa is afforded the best views.

The tented spa on the site allows day visitors, overnight guests, and villa owners to connect with themselves and the majestic landscape at the same time.

Keikoku Snow Tent
Tokyo, Japan

"It snows every winter in Hinohara village in Tokyo, and almost every year we get hit by typhoons here in Japan. We needed tents that could endure in these two rough natural conditions, and this snow tent was the one to overcome both challenges.

"After agents from the manufacturer showed me how to install them, I took part in the installment process myself. That's when I knew for sure how reliable this tent would be. We installed heat insulation walls combined with a heater – it's always warm and comfortable inside. Last but not least, the appearance of the tent looks so elegant and aesthetic!

"Thanks to the snow tent we are able to enjoy all four beautiful seasons in Tokyo."

Yuma Horikoshi

東京の檜原村はほぼ毎年雪が積もります。ここ日本に台風は毎年来ます。雪にも耐えられて、台風に耐えられるテント。このテントは、私にとって大きな課題であるこの2つの条件を満たすテントです。

メーカーの人間に建て方を教わりながら私も一緒に建てたので、よりこのテントの丈夫さを知り信頼しました。

テント内も、断熱材入りの壁にしてもらったので、エアコンをつければ、快適に過ごせます。

もちろん外観もエレガント!

このテントのおかげで、東京の春夏秋冬を存分に楽しめることができ、大変満足してます。

Kura Kura "Island of Happiness" Bali, Indonesia

The Spirit of Tri Hita Karana

"Tri Hita Karana is defined as the Three Ways to Happiness in Balinese; the harmonious trinity of humans with nature and with the spiritual.

"The spirit of Tri Hita Karana is the spirit of a world without walls. Bali is a mystical land embracing global dreamers, artists and makers; one such nomadic settler with a love for nature is Anneke van Waesberghe. She applies earth-toned eco fabric to Haute Couture Architecture; meticulously stitched and sewn to life with the geometry of love. She is our dream weaver who lives in the mountain mists of Bali.

"Poised, tranquil, pansophical is the Eco Tent on Kura Kura Bali, a room with a view perched on an island peninsula in the shape of a praying Hanoman monkey. Families, princes, scholars, Emmy-winning musicians and villagers gasp with wonder as they enter. The blue of the sky merges with the blue of the seas on an island of happiness.

Eco Tent on Kura Kura Bali is a dream – Living Without Walls.

Cherie Nursalim
Kura Kura Bali, IMAGINE Board
December 2020

Experiences

Royal High Tea

Haute Couture Architecture in a teacup, an aesthetic philosophy.

At The Sanctuary, I design the physical 'Haute Couture Architecture' of the tents, but I also design the experiences that hoteliers can provide within those tents. With intention, simple activities like afternoon tea, an afternoon at the spa and eating a meal can express the luxury of simplicity. Creating these experiences within open, flowing, tented spaces allows us to grasp the golden thread of nature and weave it into the fabric of our guests' life experience.

When drinking tea, there are no confrontations. There are discussions about daily life, what we are learning or working on, and what this life has to teach us. It's a time to enjoy the natural environment while embracing the precious moments we can spend with friends.

I started hosting informal get-togethers over tea at The Sanctuary back when I first started working with tents 20 years ago. Today that simple seed has evolved into an experience that I offer to visitors and has been picked up and used by many of my clients. I was inspired by the sophisticated simplicity of the Japanese tea ceremony, especially as expressed in *The Book of Tea* by Okakura Kakuzo. I keep that aesthetic sense, but I combine it with the more informal style of English tea. The blending of Western and Eastern cultures has a significant influence for me, and it permeates all of my designs.

The feeling should not be of mishmash or pastiche though, nor should we strip these traditions of all their integrity. Instead, we need to go back to the universal source, an intentional act of enjoying healing drinks and foods in nature in the company of friends. From there, the experience can be built up with your sense of aesthetics and philosophy. This philosophy is expressed subliminally through the objects and actions of the experience itself; for me high tea is designed to enact a conversation about sustainable design, health and well-being, craftsmanship and respect for the environment.

The slowed down, natural intentionality and increased awareness that comes along with sitting down for a cup of tea can be a great gateway to understanding the luxury of simplicity. It provides a pause within which we can strip away all of those meaningless issues which at times seem so important. We become aware of the unexpressed emotional contents, now radiating from our unattached visages. An appreciation of these simple moments and their subtle impacts sends ripples throughout the world.

The staff sets out the hand-made, imperfect, wabi-sabi style ceramic cups, wooden bowls and woven mats. Afterwards we ask the guests to sit in silence and quietly confirm a simple intention for themselves and the world around them. A gentile conversation about the tea follows. The entire ceremony should be a demonstration of caring and respect for each other and nature's wealth and beauty.This experience brings together freedom from attachments, purity of body and soul and healthy organic food, all set within a luxuriously simple aesthetic.

The Royal High Tea Ceremony and the tea set that I designed for it weave a story of the Luxury of Simplicity through the classic tea-drinking cultures of Europe, India and East Asia.

The tea box itself is a veritable laboratory of different herbs, tools, cups, spoons and teapots. We unpack it methodically as the Ceremony progesses. Each segment is opened and revealed only when it is needed. Guests enjoy the ritual of looking at the different teas, spices, herbs and the preparations required for each.

Our teas are organized according to the different doshas, taken from the Indian Ayurvedic science of health and well being. We ask a few questions so each guest can learn which dosha predominates in their own body; Kapha for the element of Earth, Vata for the element of Air, and Pitta for the element of Fire. The Tea Sommelier mixes each unique blend right there at the table, describing all of the traditional herbs that are used. My teas are grown and mixed by a friend in North Bali, who lays them out by hand to dry facing the Indian Ocean.

The handmade ceramic tea set trimmed with eco-leather.

Royal High Tea

Once the tea is prepared we sit down for snacks and conversation. The experience is slow and intentional, driven by simplicity and nature's wonder. Later in the afternoon, we play Balinese music as young dancers from the village come by to entertain our visitors. This experience brings East and West's best together in a medley of taste, aroma and culture.

The realization of the self while contemplating a cup of tea represents the vision of Haute Couture Architecture.

The Tented Tea House

The tented tea house is a space in which to be alone, have a quiet time with friends, or just enjoy the simplicity of a cup of tea. It is also a space in time to contemplate, reflect, meditate and think creatively.

Providing a space of tranquility allows guests to notice, observe, ponder and awaken to the awareness of what is taking place around and within them. The thinking mind associates with judgments, beliefs and opinions, while the meditative mind is free of these. While meditating, we are not actively engaged in thinking about any outcome. We witness the mind and stay rooted in the present.

Spa by The River

I host my spa experiences embedded in nature; in a small garden tent during the monsoons or in a 'floating tent' by the river at other times of the year. When the weather is just right, I give the more adventurous guests the option of setting up the floating tent right in the river, over the flowing water.

We start with a foot flower bath and reflexology given in comfortable chairs on the riverbank's smooth rocks. In this area, I keep alterations to the landscape to a minimum. Nature often provides a ready-made palette for us if we train ourselves to recognize it. Because the flat rocks on the river shore continue and submerge slightly into the water, they provide calm water and a flat space for the massage tables. The therapists love this unusual practice of giving a traditional Balinese massage over the cool water, while the guests can see the river passing by from the peek hole in the head pillow. Our guests are lulled into a dream state by the soft sights and sounds of nature as they watch the water passing by. When the massage is finished, guests are served a fresh juice tea and are left to silent contemplation as the sun slowly sinks beyond the horizon.

Nature often provides a ready-made palette for us if we train ourselves to recognize it.

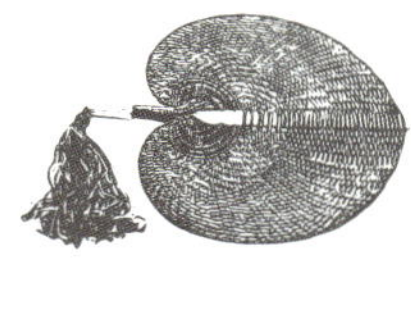

> *"May what I do flow from me like a river, no forcing and no holding back, the way it is with children."*

Rainer Maria Rilke

On the banks
of a river slow
life returns
with steady resolve

unhurried unrushed
time pauses
as veils shrubs foster

your worries your life
YOU
overtaken
by the calm riverside
silently accepting your grudges
and sidestepping your ego
just the river
and you
one with the flowers
and the bees

Poem by Adi

The Outpost tent can be used as a spa, an office, a space for meditation or a tea house, depending on my needs.

The floating tent hangs freely in the air from three bamboo poles, creating a soft and soothing spa setting.

Dining With Intent

Whether they're for guests, myself or old friends, my dining experiences are about touching the six senses: teasing the palette, wafting fresh scents to the nostrils, creating a feast for the eyes, allowing the sounds of nature to enter the space, having the pleasure of feeling the wooden table and linen table cloth; altogether creating the sense and awareness of being within an intentional space.

The canvas panels are rolled up to let the dense foliage and endless views of nature come inside, this is the art of Living Without Walls, after all. I also make sure the lush greenery is brought to the table; it might be simple banana leaves on the plate settings or fresh cut vines wrapped around the wood and camp lantern chandelier.

I serve mostly lightly cooked fresh vegetables from the organic garden, garnished with local chilies, ginger, garlic and coconut in our modern take on traditional Balinese recipes. My guests come expecting this experience and I can see from their faces that it satisfies more than a complex presentation in a closed-off setting ever could. If we serve meat, it is always fresh and free-range from the local villages; we want our respect for the food and the people who make it come through on the plate.

As the meal comes to a close, the entire table sits back in peace, enjoying a glass of wine, listening to the wind rustling in the palm trees, the gentle murmuring of the river and the crickets chirping in the foliage.

Picnics at The Sanctuary

I believe in keeping the old-world luxury of laying down peacefully on a sunny afternoon in the middle of nature. This is the luxury that I strive to bring to my guests at The Sanctuary; the luxury of being able to take their time enjoying a light meal, reclining on rattan carpets and pillows by the river, listening to the tropical forest, letting the surroundings stage their dreams while their bodies readjust to the natural rhythms of the ancient jungle.

I have some spaces near the water and the smooth river rocks, and others up on the terraces overlooking the small valley. It depends on the guest, the weather and what kind of mood I want to invoke.

Time to oneself is also a luxury. My guests need to feel free and at leisure with nature and their selves. They are free and encouraged to climb the rocks, look for birds and wildlife, watch the sway of the rice fields and banana leaves in the breeze, or just sit in easy conversation.

On the grassy river bank,
We place our tartan rug upon the ground.
The gently flowing river and random birdsong,
Are the only audible sounds.

We sit down on the rug and relax,
Basking in the glorious sunshine.
Then open our wicker picnic basket,
To reveal food and drink on which we'll dine.

There's plenty for us all to share,
Including a gorgeous home-made savoury tart.
There's also finger food and various fruits,
And, in no time at all, we all make a start.

We've brought a bottle of Champagne,
For a special treat, for us all to drink.
I love to watch the tiny bubbles rise.
'Cheers! ' we exclaim, as, together, our glasses clink.

As we sit, a sudden movement catches my eye;
I see a fleeting flash of vivid bright blue.
To my joy, I realise it's a kingfisher,
On the look out for his daily food.

Nearby, I spot some dragonflies,
Darting quickly here and there.
At their lovely, iridescent colours,
I can't help but sit and stare.

There are many beautiful butterflies;
In the air, they dance round together.
They chase each other to and fro,
Coaxed out by this lovely weather.

A pair of swans swim serenely by;
Their feathers are as white as snow.
I marvel at their amazing majesty,
As I watch them onwardly go.

The river, as it gently flows,
Is a haven and a duck's delight.
They seem happy and contented,
As they swim in the sunshine so bright.

As we sit there laughing and relaxing,
We're cooled by a delicious breeze.
We don't seem to have a care in the world.
Oh! How I adore days just like these!

Days like these are so very precious,
And they're always such good fun.
I sit there reclining, lost in thought,
As I tuck in to a sticky Belgian Bun.

The afternoon draws to a close,
And we all pack our things away.
With the current run of glorious weather,
We're bound to return another day.

Picnic by the River, Angela Wybrow

VI.

Haute Couture Architecture Inspirations

"Bridging the gap between nature and architecture"

Living Without Walls

Living Outside the Box

Living With Intent

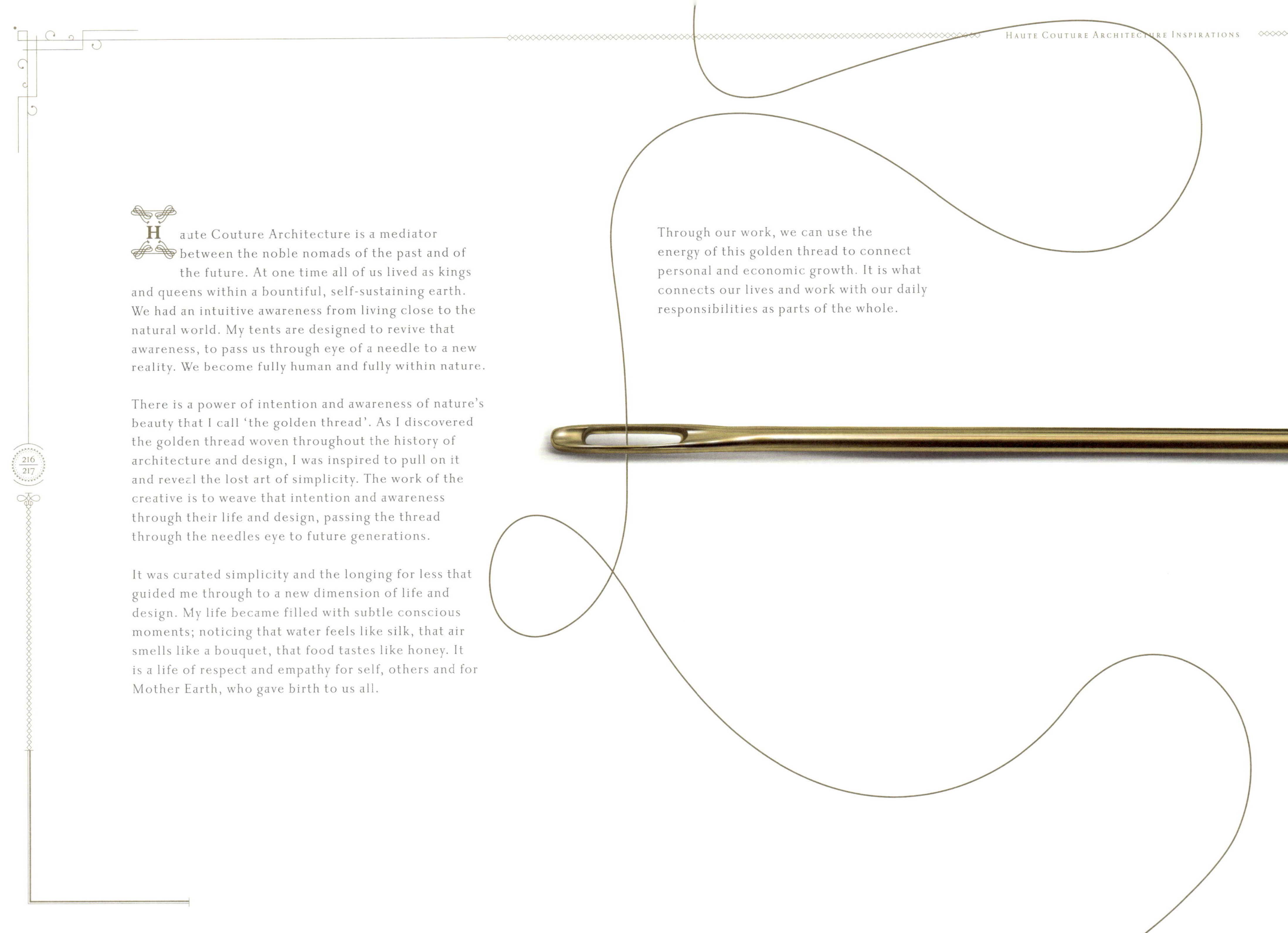

Haute Couture Architecture is a mediator between the noble nomads of the past and of the future. At one time all of us lived as kings and queens within a bountiful, self-sustaining earth. We had an intuitive awareness from living close to the natural world. My tents are designed to revive that awareness, to pass us through eye of a needle to a new reality. We become fully human and fully within nature.

There is a power of intention and awareness of nature's beauty that I call 'the golden thread'. As I discovered the golden thread woven throughout the history of architecture and design, I was inspired to pull on it and reveal the lost art of simplicity. The work of the creative is to weave that intention and awareness through their life and design, passing the thread through the needles eye to future generations.

It was curated simplicity and the longing for less that guided me through to a new dimension of life and design. My life became filled with subtle conscious moments; noticing that water feels like silk, that air smells like a bouquet, that food tastes like honey. It is a life of respect and empathy for self, others and for Mother Earth, who gave birth to us all.

Through our work, we can use the energy of this golden thread to connect personal and economic growth. It is what connects our lives and work with our daily responsibilities as parts of the whole.

While the inspirations for Haute Couture Architecture spread out like ripples spread through space and time, they were discovered personally at various turning points throughout my own life. I am continually inspired by what I see around me, what I experience, and the exciting works of other designers worldwide. Some influences stand out above all others though; the vegetal twisting patterns and awareness of nature in the art nouveau movement, the honest, refined simplicity of Wabi-Sabi design philosophy, the clean lines and framing of nature seen in early modernism and Frank Lloyd Wright, and the idea of ephemerally draping the landscape in the earthworks art of Christo and Jeanne-Claude.

In my own life, I worked intensively to explore the meeting of Eastern and Western ideas in design philosophy, and created Design For the Environment principles to reduce manufacturing waste and create lasting, sustainably produced products. These ideas are also central to my work up to this day.

Haute Couture Architecture took shape while I lived in Bali, so the vernacular architecture of this island and the philosophies embedded in it have also been very influential to me and my design.

Finally, because I work with tents and design for the modern Global Nomads, the history of tented architecture and the development of biophilic materials that imitate natural processes also play a large part in my creations.

Every new idea is interwoven with those that came before it. Haute Couture Architecture is filled with blissful ideas of simplicity, love of nature, shared humanity, living with intention and living with attention to the planet as a whole.

Art Nouveau

Whiplash motifs at Vitebsky railway station by Sima Mihash and Stanislav Brzozowski, Saint Petersburg 1904.

Four of the most important domesticated silk moths. *Meyers Konversations-Lexikon.*

Gate in Gothenburg, Sweden. Photo by Camilla Engman.

Flower shop in Brussels, designed by Paul Hanker.

Design by Rafael Maso for the La Gabarra factory in La Bisbal d'Emporda, Catalonia, Spain.

Stairway and skylight of the Horta Museum.

In the 1970s and early 80s I was living in Brussels, Belgium. While there, I was profoundly influenced by the curved organic forms on the old Art Nouveau buildings throughout the city. I think of the Art Nouveau movement as a sparkling crystal, reflecting a love of nature through the lens of art and design. The Art Nouveau style inspired me because of its talented artists, designers and architects. Originally coming via Japan in the late 19th century, it transcended and moved across Europe's borders. It was a dynamic movement.

Over time, we have built a smoother, mechanical world over the elaborate past, but these beautiful Art Nouveau buildings with their twisting vines and flowers still stand out. They pay tribute to a symbolism that goes back to the ancient world, a world that can still be sensed when visiting the former home of architect Victor Horta, now the Horta Museum, in Brussels. Horta's Tassel House, built in 1893, is often considered the first Art Nouveau building because of its highly innovative plan and groundbreaking use of materials and decoration.

Spiral Staircase of the Tassel House with its whiplash curved lines, Brussels, by Victor Horta.

Mariano Fortuny y Madrazo (1871-1949) brought Art Nouveau concepts to fabric and dress design, reflecting the flows and curves of the period's architecture and arts. Carrying the Japanese aesthetic influence onto clothing, he worked with silks and kimono-inspired fabrics.

Fortuny Madrazo was one of the most creative minds of his time. He mainly worked in Italy, and was renowned for his Art Nouveau textiles, including fine-pleated silk gowns, lustrous silks, and velvet scarves.

The pleats of the Fortuny tea gown, modelled by Mrs. Conde Nast in the image on the left, reflect the patterns found in nature as photographed by Karl Blossfeldt in the center image. The same flowing lines and inspiration from nature and the classical world are reflected on the facade of the Maison Cauchie by Paul Cauchie, shown on the right.

The natural patterns and folded style of the Fortuny dress on the left show direct inspiration from Japanese design, as illustrated in the center print, *A Flower Game in the Garden*, by Utagawa Kunisada. The same appreciation for nature comes out in the art deco apartment facade and balconies by Gustave Strauven on the right.

Macro images by Karl Blossfeldt 1923.

> *"A plant must be valued as an artistic and architectural structure."*
>
> Karl Blossfeldt

I was also inspired by the profound passion for nature shown in the works of Karl Blossfeldt. Blossfeldt was a photographer, sculptor, teacher and artist who worked in Berlin, Germany, during the same period as Horta and his contemporaries. His close-up images help us see images we wouldn't see with our bare eyes through the camera's lens. Seeds, leaves and stems appear as abstract figures or alien creatures. The way they have been photographed, they come to us as swirling sculptural objects and forms as they are found in nature, frozen in time.

Cucurbita (a gourd) by Karl Blossfeldt, a German photographer.

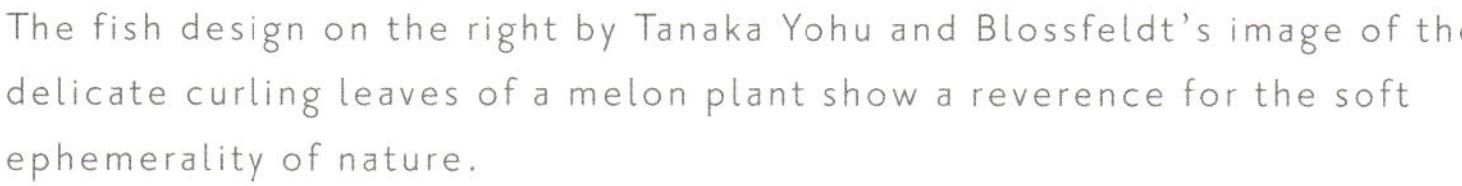

The fish design on the right by Tanaka Yohu and Blossfeldt's image of the delicate curling leaves of a melon plant show a reverence for the soft ephemerality of nature.

A significant event in the history of the West was the discovery of Eastern cultures. In Art Nouveau, it was specifically the Japanese and their focus on nature and religion rather than materialism that drove a change in design consciousness.

While studying the Art Nouveau movement with its artists and designers, I became obsessed with the Japanese artworks that had inspired them. In 1985 I planned to organize an exhibition in Tokyo to showcase the links between Art Nouveau and Japanese arts and craft, inviting and hosting researchers from all around Japan. During our discussions with Japanese translators, we were able to confirm and expand many of my findings.

In 1982 while I was organizing the exhibition, East Meets West, the Belgian Ambassador in Tokyo took pride in this initiative and took over the project after I left Tokyo to finalize my research. I introduced him to the Director of the Palais des Beaux-Arts in Brussels, the museum built by Victor Horta, where I temporarily held office. The exhibition attracted attention from governments and architects such as Kenzo Tange, Shigeru Ban, Norman Foster, and designers such as Massimo Vignelli.

That same year, I discovered the *Great Encyclopedia of Yedo* by Takashima Hokkai. Takashima was an accomplished artist, as well as a trained botanist and forester. His forestry work earned him a government-sponsored three-year mission to Nancy, France, in the 1880s, where he attended the École Forestière courses.

Knowing how to reconcile tradition and novelty, Takashima was a painter with talent full of finesse and sensitivity. He arrived in France with a personal art collection with which he soon triggered the local artistic circle's interest, including such contemporaries as Emile Galle, Louis Hestaux, Camille Martin and René Wiener.

Because Japan had been closed off from the rest of the world during the Meiji period, any foreign influence was almost non-existent in Takashima's collection. His French contemporaries were lucky to be exposed to those treasures of Japanese art and Takashima's artistic style, as he had an aura with which the West was not yet familiar.

When he returned to Japan, Takashima left ninety-eight of his paintings to René Wiener and left numerous plates to the Forestry School.

After meeting Takashima Hokkai, Emile Gallè became one of the driving forces and major innovators behind the Art Nouveau movement. His naturalistic designs and innovative techniques made him one of the pioneering glassmakers of the late 19th and early 20th centuries.

Takashima Hokkai as drawn by Edmond Auguin.

Drawings from the collection of botanist Takashima Hokkai depicted on vases designed by Emile Gallè.

Gallè had an extensive flower garden at his residence, which he used as a source of models for his Japanese influenced art.

Gallè was also a furniture designer. In the article *Contemporary Furniture Decorated Following Nature* he argued that true beauty could never be found "in the acceptance of the falseness and mediocrity of prettiness without character or opulence without spirit". He stated that beauty could only be found in the concentrated application of the principles of structural and linear growth of nature. In following this doctrine, every detail and motif in his furniture was taken directly from natural forms.

The Art Nouveau movement itself grew to be characterized by its use of long, curved, organic lines employed in architecture, interior design, jewelry and glass design, posters, and illustration.

The furniture pieces by Emile Galle, above, bring the curving life of nature to stationary objects.

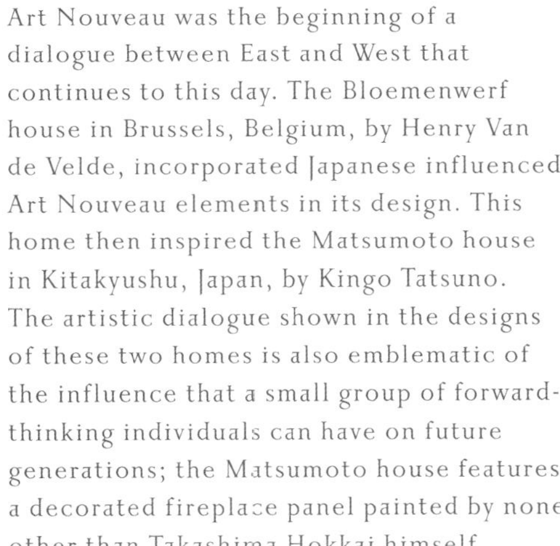

Art Nouveau was the beginning of a dialogue between East and West that continues to this day. The Bloemenwerf house in Brussels, Belgium, by Henry Van de Velde, incorporated Japanese influenced Art Nouveau elements in its design. This home then inspired the Matsumoto house in Kitakyushu, Japan, by Kingo Tatsuno. The artistic dialogue shown in the designs of these two homes is also emblematic of the influence that a small group of forward-thinking individuals can have on future generations; the Matsumoto house features a decorated fireplace panel painted by none other than Takashima Hokkai himself.

Images at the top and bottom left show the home of Matsumoto Kenjiro, designed by Kingo Tatsuno. Images at the top and bottom right show the home of architect Henry Van De Velde.

After Takashima Hokkai returned to Japan, his floral motifs started to show the influence of the artistic milieu that he was a part of in France, as seen in this fireplace wall for the Matsumoto house.

My own arched walls were inspired by this image, now recombined with canvas and Balinese bamboo, the painted flowers replaced by living ones.

> *"The mission of art is not to copy nature, but to express it!"*
>
> Honoré De Balzac (Tours 1799-Paris 1850)

Magnolia Lamp made by Louis Majorelle at the Daum brothers.

Magnolia, also known as white sandalwood or jade orchid.

The Fig is generosity.

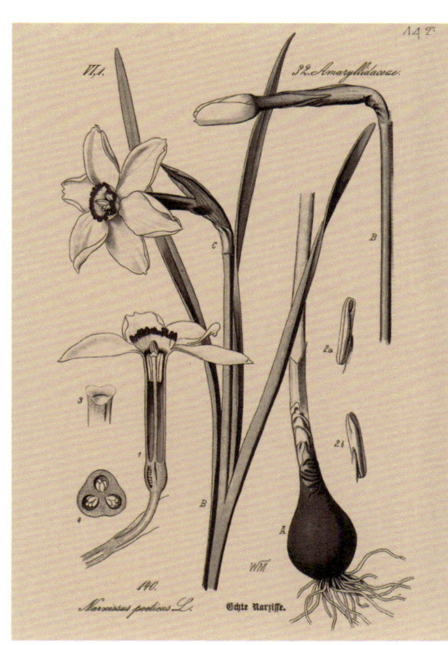

The Narcissus is springtime in nature.

The Myrtle is joy.

Emile Galle wrote in 1893 that according to Saint Paul, each flower and fruit had a particular symbolic meaning:

- *The Grape is the symbol of the Eucharist*
- *The Fig is generosity*
- *The Veronica flower is fidelity*
- *The Myrtle is joy*
- *The Narcissus is springtime in nature*
- *The olive leaf is peace*
- *Wheat is charity & goodness*

Japonaiserie by Vincent van Gogh.

Japanese print on wood with seal motifs by Rene Wiener, the Takashima Hokkai Collection.

Die Hoffnung II by Gustav Klimt, Museum of Modern Art, New York.

Wabi-Sabi

Through my travels and work in Japan, I became exposed to the Wabi-Sabi philosophy and aesthetic, which profoundly influenced my understanding of simplicity in design and lifestyle.

Wabi-sabi is the view, or thought, of finding beauty in the very imperfections created by nature. It is the aesthetic of things in existence; imperfect, impermanent, incomplete and transient. It is an irregularity, rawness, simplicity, economy, soberness, humbleness, intimacy, an appreciation of natural objects and processes. It invites us to go deeper and celebrate that fragile and raw reality.

If you live the Wabi-Sabi lifestyle, it can lift you from the stress of daily life, letting you be happy with who you are and what you can achieve when you lie low.

I have been called the perfect perfectionist, which I take as a compliment. However, some of our mistakes have ultimately turned out to be some of the best work we have ever made. When we want to live our lives to the fullest and with the least obstruction from our inside and outside worlds, the Wabi-Sabi attitude of accepting the inherent beauty within what might otherwise be seen as a flaw or a mistake is something that deserves close attention.

Bark of the coconut tree.

Bark of a palm tree.

Wabi-Sabi inspired floating tent.

The Wabi-Sabi house is not just about simplicity; it also attaches a sense of calm. When you want to bring Wabi-Sabi's life force into your house, you also bring outdoor properties (such as plants, wood and stone) inside. These elements are part of our survival, and the peace and harmony they create foster a sense of belonging and creativity.

Wabi-Sabi is also about repurposing, reclaiming and reusing things you already have. You save money by using old things in new and creative ways. These objects make you even happier because you created them.

This concept is deeply embedded in my beliefs of how we should take care of the environment and create changes to make a better world. Wabi-Sabi recreates the old and invites the beholder to admire its beauty.

> *“But when does something’s destiny finally come to fruition? Is the plant complete when it flowers? When it goes to seed? When the seeds sprout? When everything turns into compost?”*
>
> Leonard Koren

The Wabi-Sabi attitude is about enjoying each process of aging and seeing its beauty. If you can see the increased attractiveness of an old leather suitcase or the fading of colors in a fabric pattern, you can understand Wabi-Sabi. If you can appreciate the weathering and discoloring of wood, or the aging of a leaf, you experience Wabi-Sabi.

Broken earth clay pot with ashes from hardwooc to make lye for producing home-made soap.

Mishima ware hakeme type tea bowl with kintsugi gold lacquer, 16th century Japan (Ethnological Museum of Berlin).

Wabi-Sabi does not glorify an imaginary realm with fantastical imagery. It does not even point to geometric perfection. Instead, it highlights the texture, decay, fragility and complexity of Mother Nature as she shines through humanity's works. The experiencer passes through the eye of the needle via the experience itself; rough floorboards, chipped pottery and coarse cloth all point to an unseen force that both corrupts and uplifts human creations.

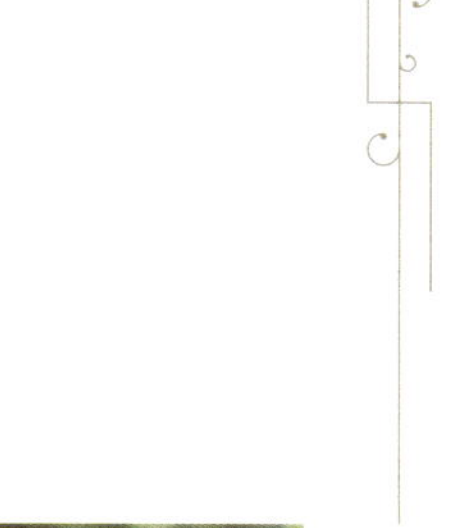

Japanese Raku Technique.

East Meets West in Design

In the 1980s, I formed an organization that was aimed at fostering cross-cultural communication between Japanese and Western designers, called East Meets West Cultural International. At that time, the idea was so novel that an article about my work felt a need to mention "the difficulty of bridging cultural differences" and that our work brought "creative fields, not to mention cultures together, which have not always been the most comfortable of soul mates". Despite the news headlines, the world of 2020 is much more connected and at peace culturally than most could even imagine just 30 years ago.

Even then, though, I could see that the force of modernism and modernization would one day create a world in which it was (almost) impossible to distinguish between a Western or Eastern designer's work. We have opened up new vistas in terms of incorporating disparate philosophies and ideas into our work. However, I encourage young designers not to lose track of their cultural influences and the integrity that they create. We should create authentic dialogue and diversity rather than homogeneity.

East Meets West sponsored a design competition that, at that time, was unlike any other; we proposed to create a design aesthetic that reflected the fusion of cross-cultural ideas and influences between Japan and the West. To do some we solicited entries in five separate categories: Applied Arts and Crafts, Architecture, Graphic Art and Package Design, Industrial Design and Interior Design.

The following images and text are from my accompanying book, *East Meets West in Design: Archeology of the Present*. In today's world we see international design styles mixed freely, however these quality pieces have stood the test of time.

Tamiko Kawata Ferguson, USA.

"Alphabet Spoons A to E", 1987. 5 spoons; Tea Sugar, Hors d'oeuvre, Demitasse, Bar, sterling silver. "Metal flatware wasn't generally used in Japan until after the Second World War when spoons became particularly popular. I used the alphabet's letters A to E as a motif to design these spoons. The Japanese tradition of simplicity in forms and finishes, and playfulness with practical items translates a Western utensil for the Eastern table."

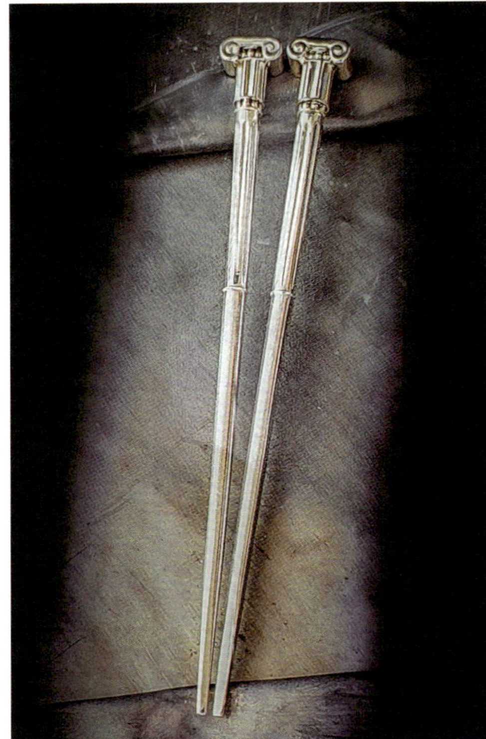

Trudy Borenstein-Sugiura, USA. "Ionic Chopsticks", 1988. Sterling silver.

"An important part of the Japanese dining experience is presentation, with elaborate thought given to the color, shape and texture of foods, as well as settings. The Ionic Chopsticks are made in sterling silver, traditional material for Western fine dining utensils. This design combines a classic symbol of Western culture with a shape and dimension of Japanese dining The fine craftsmanship of the chopsticks themselves, speak of the attention to detail on a small scale that we have come to associate with Japanese production in the late 20th century. In making a traditionally disposable Eastern utensil out of a precious material, the artist comments wryly on the sushi invasion rampant in Western cities today. Topping the Eastern dining tool with a classical, Western column order, adds another level of depth into the breath between East and West. It is a product that either culture would find both simultaneously comforting and disturbing. This tension is highly stimulating."

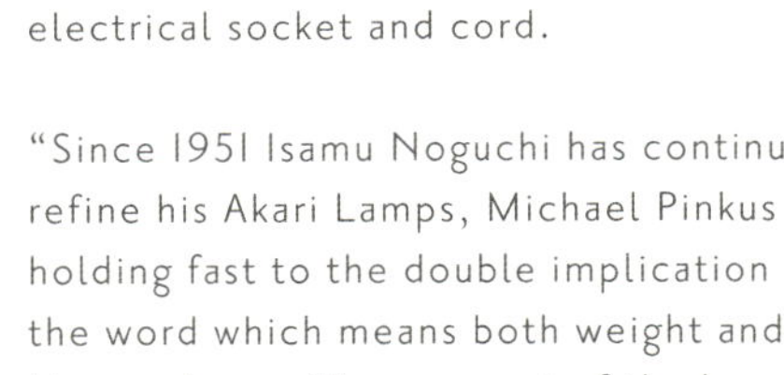

Michael Pinkus, USA. "The Hanger Lamp", 1987. Paper coated wire hangers, acrylic feet, electrical socket and cord.

"Since 1951 Isamu Noguchi has continued to refine his Akari Lamps, Michael Pinkus USA, holding fast to the double implication of the word which means both weight and The Hanger Lamp. The concept of the hanger lamp intends to mirror these same qualities. The lamp made from three metal hangers, those so well-known paper covered from the dry cleaners, yield an object whose minimalism and elegance strive to approach the evanescent qualities of a Noguchi's Akari Lamp. Both process and product become an expression of an aesthetic generally reserved for a precious craft. This piece shows how different and similar the two cultures are."

Hermann Becker West Germany. "Backrest", 1987. Chair welded steel, felt.

"Sitting, which is a simple matter of comfort in the West, is still inspired by the spirit of an inner consciousness of form in the East. The traditional Japanese sitting room doesn't require furniture in the Western sense, as the empty room is regarded as a shaping in itself. The backrest takes up this experience."

Me modeling the return to Japonism in 20th century fashion design.

Bengt Rodell, Sweden. "Europanese Drinking Cup", 1988. Glass and plastic.

"The sake cup, an ancient Japanese cultural object, meets the Western drinking glass, and a new drinking cup is born."

Raimund Erdmann, Switzerland. "MA: a furniture piece to house a collection", 1984. Cherry and maple wood.

"While working in Japan I encountered another way of thinking about space that extends beyond the three dimensions of thoughts of time and space, between inside and outside, or between questions and answers. I tried to capture this understanding of MA in this piece of furniture. The supporting structure of the drawers reaches beyond the column defining a frame above, thus creating a space both inside and outside the collection."

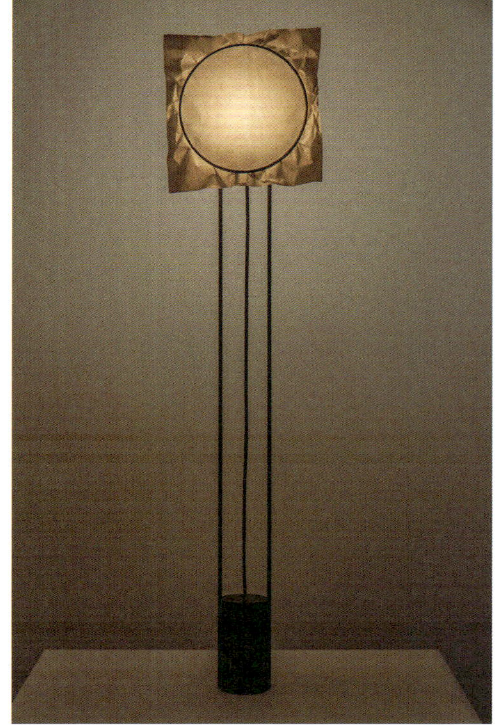

V.Lorenzo Porcelli, USA. "Porcelli Corona Floor Lamp", 1981. Painted steel structure, solid aluminum base, handmade Japanese rice paper shade.

"A confluence of cultures can be seen contributing to the design character of this lamp. The first mock-up was in wood and seemed to reflect two cultures– the Shaker, (simple wood forms), and the Japanese, (handmade rice paper, the circle). To make it more international in character and Compete with lighting designs from Europe, it took on the Italian culture, (satin black enamelled steel)."

Julia Lyon, U.S.A. "Container - Service Tools -Tasting Cup", 1987. Teapot, Pot and Serving tools; scooper, spreader pick. Hand forged sterling silver alloy, ebony.

"The finish is in keeping with the traditional use of low luster white metal vessels for Senchado saki and tea ceremonies in Shinto Shrines. One of my concerns is to surprise the user. The three hand- forged service tools stored in the handle of the container serve this purpose."

Contrast and Harmony, by Shigeru Ban

"I've never been interested in luxury fashion brands, and I've never been in a store to take a closer look at the products. However, Renzo Piano asked me to create an exhibition pavilion for the first time of the new brand "Hermès Maison", a new brand of housing-related products such as Hermès furniture, which will be debuted in Milano Salone. I was introduced to Hermès officials at his office and decided to seriously study this brand.

First of all, at the Hermes atelier in the suburb of Paris, I was shown the site where leather craftsmen actually made bags. Until I saw it, I imagined a place like a modern factory that was mechanized to some extent, but in reality there was no machine at all. All the work was done by hand and each craftsman was responsible for one bag through every process. It was a true non-modern 'atelier' and I was overwhelmed by the skills, spirit and pride of the craftsmen. Of course, the furniture that were going to be exhibited this time were also made by the same process. How should we display these products which are the harmony of high-leveled materials, design, and technology? Also, this pavilion was required to be relocated to cities such as Tokyo, New York, and Shanghai after its debut in Milan."

The Hermès Maison tent pavilion, by Shigeru Ban.

"Therefore, I thought about an exhibition-space system that keeps 'contrast and harmony' with the exhibited items. It was meaningless to create an exhibition system only contrasting the details and materials of the furniture, such as luxury leather or high-quality wood, in terms of cost and my usual method. I also learned through my architectural experiences that the quality of wonderful spaces has nothing to do with the quality of the materials that make them up. Therefore, I used recycled paper tubes that I always use as to contrast with the materials of high-class products, gave them various thicknesses and densities, and created a delicate combination that makes it look as if they were knitted, creating harmony with Hermès products by weaving light and shadow through the pattern.

Considering transportation to several places, we used four different diameters of paper tubes so that thinner tubes could be nested in thicker ones, and bundled them with horizontal plywood boards to give strength. The paper tubes and the boards were joined by inserting thin wooden rod-shaped pins crossing at the top and bottom of the shelves to facilitate assembly and disassembly."

Modern Architecture

Fallingwater (Kaufmann Residence) by Frank Lloyd Wright. The house was built partly over a waterfall on Bear Run, in the Mill Run section of Stewart Township, Fayette County, Pennsylvania.

Frank Lloyd Wright brought us from Art Nouveau to early Modernism, via Art Deco and Arts and Crafts. I think of him as the greatest of the early moderns. He thought of interior & exterior spaces as one, was ahead of his time in building forms and construction methods, and never went to a formal architecture school.

In his Millard house, we can see indoor spaces flowing to the outdoor and even suggest the seemingly wild courtyard gardens found in traditional Japanese design.

Another modernist influence on my own design (not necessarily in aesthetics but in philosophy) is R. Buckminster Fuller, who saw that working towards an increasingly light footprint should be our future. He felt that the "accelerating acceleration" of the modern world would eventually lead to "ephemeralization", as technology allowed us to do "more and more with less and less until eventually you can do everything with nothing". His unique Dymaxion house also presaged today's emerging global nomads, a new society very similar to what he had imagined back then.

Modern architecture eventually covered the world in glass, steel and concrete structures that cared nothing for nature. Many early moderns, however, celebrated the living world. They embedded their structures and designs in nature, and used Her natural efficiency to inspire their engineering.

Earthworks Art

In the 1980s, I was an avid art collector and was lucky enough to spend my days and nights among the artistic milieu of Manhattan. In my work of fabric-draped constructions, I have been greatly influenced by the work of Christo and Jeanne-Claude. Their temporary environmental installations bring us closer to the natural environment, inspire wonder and open the mind to new possibilities.

In an interview Christo stated: "I am an artist, and I have to have courage. Do you know that I don't have any artworks that exist? They all go away when they're finished. Only the preparatory drawings and collages are left, giving my works an almost legendary character. I think it takes much greater courage to create things to be gone than to create things that will remain."

Christo and Jeanne-Claude. *Running Fence*, Sonoma and Marin Counties, California 1972-76; ©Christo; Color photograph by Jeanne-Claude, 1976.

Like Wabi-Sabi masters, Christo and Jeanne-Claude understood that the human experience, though impossible to grasp or touch, is more potent than any other force.

Their earthworks installations are ephemeral and ambiguous. By warping, wrapping, and transforming a landscape, they force us to engage with that landscape. The Running Fence is not spectacular because it is a fence, but because it wakes us up to experience the landscape that it intersects.

Viewing the Wrapped Reichstag, the very absence of the building forced us to confront the entirety of our experience associated with it. When wrapped up in fabrics, we realized that the real Reichstag was inside our minds and our collective experience, not in the building. Both Christo and Jeanne-Claude's The Gates and Balinese temple doorways are not doorways to a physical building but an experience. They blur the boundaries between the inside and outside. The boundary is between the human as a subjective observer, and the human as a part of the invisible world of nature. If we are open to the unseen, The Gates allow us to physically walk through the eye of the needle.

The Gates. Exhibition Period—February 12th through 27th 2005. 7,503 Gates ran over 23 miles of walkways in Central Park, New York; each gate was 16 feet high, with widths varying according to the paths' width. ©2005 Christo and Jeanne-Claude, Photo by Wolfgang Volz.

The Gates. Exhibition Period—February 12th through 27th 2005. © 2005 Christo and Jeanne-Claude. Photo by Wolfgang Volz.

Besakih temple in Bali, Indonesia. Photo by Joana Kruse.

Design for the Environment

I grew up in Holland during the 1950s and '60s. My mother, a teenager during the Second World War, always repeated the mantra "save, save, save". We learned to turn off the lights when we left the room, not to throw away food, not to let the water run, et cetera. She learned these things out of necessity, but as I grew older and became aware of environmental issues, these early influences guided me to a simpler and less resource-intensive lifestyle. For the sake of nature and the planet, this mantra should be repeated by all of us.

In 1992 I developed a set of guidelines for a design competition hosted by my organization, East Meets West. The guidelines were to act as a template for Design For the Environment (DFE) protocols, which designers could use to reduce the impact the products they designed had on nature. These ideas have become so accepted that some of the guidelines, such as "using raw materials that include only renewable and sustainable resources", have become commonplace. At the time, however, they were ground-breaking enough for me to be interviewed on television and magazines to explain the concept.

Despite this progress, however, many of the DFE guidelines are even more foreign to today's cheap manufacturing and one-time use design than they were in the world of the 1990s. I am still concerned with not only what goes into a product but about its lifecycle process.

Why Design for the Environment? Eliminating or reducing environmental problems requires a fundamental shift in society, one in which designers have an essential role. When designers select materials to be used in a product, they determine whether sustainable resources are used, how much energy will be consumed during production, what pollutants will be generated, and how the product will be disposed of or potentially recycled or reused. The throwaway society uses so much energy, emits so much carbon and generates so much air pollution, acid rain, water pollution, toxic waste and rubbish that it is strangling itself. The problem of overflowing landfills is just one consequence of a wasteful society. Producing conventional products and packaging takes an enormous toll on the earth's limited resources and generates tremendous amounts of pollution.

The choices we make as designers have a significant impact on the environment. Producing steel from scrap rather than iron ore cuts water pollution by 85%, energy use by two thirds, and eliminates mining wastes. A refillable glass bottle that is used ten times consumes 90% less energy than some single-use containers. Many of these changes are very simple; for example, I remember a case whereby a small alteration in the cord of a computer mouse, eliminated 87% of the packaging used.

Other changes are more complex, such as BMW's development of a car whose parts could easily be disassembled and reused, shown on the next page. The industries that are now addressing environmental issues are finding that the benefits can exceed the cost. They save money in production and waste disposal, get a jump on new regulations and gain recognition as "good corporate citizens". Designers who develop innovative products are challenging the myth that products that are safer for the environment are expensive and unattractive.

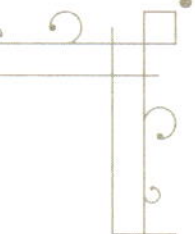

With exterior body cladding of a GE thermoplastic alloy over a metal chassis, the BMW Z1 was a classic example of Design for Disassembly in the late '80s. Every exterior panel could be replaced when necessary.

Design for the Environment Guidelines for Products

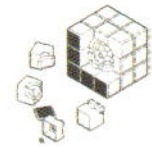

- *Designed for disassembly and reuse, easy maintenance, or recycling and reuse.*

- *Avoids the use of toxic or environmentally harmful materials, glues, adhesives, coatings, stabilizers.*

- *Uses less material or the size, and weight is reduced to facilitate energy efficiency in the transportation of raw materials or finished products.*
- *Designed for a long life-span.*

- *Saves energy during manufacture, distribution, and use.*

- *Uses materials that are recycled or can be easily recycled.*

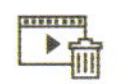

- *Estimated percentage of maximum potential recycled content.*

- *Uses materials derived from renewable resources.*

- *Uses single resin materials.*
- *Designed for easy repair or refurbishment.*

- *Designed for a second life.*

- *Considers consumer safety.*

- *Does not use endangered plants or animals or scarce resources.*

- *Materials are locally or regionally available.*

- *Raw material extraction does not disturb sensitive ecosystems or cultures.*

- *Assembly or manufacture does not negatively affect communities and makes use of existing infrastructures.*

Lifecycle of a tent

Tent Fabrics Re-purpose

After 10 years roof fabrics collected

Repurposing tent fabrics into strong shopping bags

Fabrics are shredded and recycled

Woven into a new fabric

Tomorrow | *Today*

Tent Frame: Cradle to Cradle

Manufacturing tent frames

After 25 years refurbish the frames, ideally with upcycled fabrics to create new tents

Recycle the steel

Scrap dealer

Escape Nomade tents can be fully disassembled in a few hours, re-installed in one day and re-used or recycled after their 25 year lifecycle.

Design for the Environment Guidelines for Packaging

✣ *The packaging is eliminated or incorporated as part of the product design and use.*

✣ *Uses non-toxic inks, glues, adhesives, coatings, stabilizers.*

✣ *Uses a minimal amount of materials to fulfill a function.*

✣ *Uses primarily materials that are recycled or be easily recycled.*

✣ *The estimated potential recycled content percentage.*

✣ *Materials are homogeneous or need not be further separated before recycling.*

✣ *Avoids the use of toxic or hazardous materials.*

✣ *Uses no materials derived from endangered or scarce resources.*

✣ *Containers are refillable or reusable.*

✣ *Materials are lightweight.*

✣ *Incorporates functional reuse after primary use expired.*

✣ *Raw material extraction does not disturb sensitive ecosystems or cultures.*

✣ *Considers consumer safety.*

✣ *Coarse materials include only renewable and sustainable resources.*

✣ *Labels, seals, and closures are compatible with recycling systems.*

I use durable materials with a long life span for my designs. I design for disassembly; the owners of my tents can replace parts without replacing the entire product. Design that considers repair and replacement parts is unfortunately even less common today than in the 1990s. However, it is just as crucial as using sustainable and recyclable materials.

I use sustainably grown and harvested solid teak wood for my furniture, held together with minimal but high-quality heavy-duty hardware. Using high-quality materials ensures a longer lifespan and gives the user the ability to repair and replace single components.

Our fabrics have an eight-year limited warranty from the manufacturer, one of the highest in the industry. Each wall panel and roof layer can be replaced individually so that only small parts of the building need to be replaced. Typical tent manufacturers using less durable materials will go the other way, opting for a single stitched covering that must be replaced in its entirety. They gain revenue by producing replacement parts, but it comes at a considerable cost to the environment. I opt to reach a target market that prefers long term cost savings and leaving a smaller footprint on the earth over cheaper, less durable products.

The next consideration is the energy that will be used by the product. In construction and architecture, this often comes under the term, Bioclimatic Design. It is common to see a modern building that generates internal heat through large glass windows, then cooled down by air conditioning. In our tents, we provide insulation, just as in a standard building. What's different from a standard building (and many tents) is that we designed walls that can simply be rolled up, allowing natural cooling. The roof comes in four layers, which allows the hot air to naturally filter up and escape through the eaves, while the harshness of the sun's rays is deflected away. In tropical locations, we also position the tents for cross ventilation and the flow of cool air.

The art of packaging vegetables with banana leaves.

Biophilia

Nature is mysterious,
It is an other;
it is a void onto which we project our fears,
hopes, and dreams.

Biophilia, the simple yet extravagant love of nature, is stitched through my work and the work of those who have inspired me. Although the term was uncommon when I started designing my products, the idea is primary to my aesthetic.

Plants, animals and humans all share common DNA. We humans even share 60% of ours with bananas. There is more that connects us to the natural world than divides us from it. However, the natural world is often made invisible; instead we prefer to live in a made-up world of human ideas and relationships.

I strive to make this invisible world present through my designs by creating a balanced flow between indoor and outdoor spaces. I want to sit in the open-walled living area of my tents and enjoy vistas that reach as far as the eye can see. I want to be immersed in the theater of nature.

The green panorama of ancient trees, yellow bamboo and tall native grasses is all framed by the bamboo poles covering the tent frames.

From my living area in The Sanctuary, I just have to glance over to see the farmers working in the rice fields, fishermen by the river and monkeys climbing trees. The birds and butterflies sometimes fly through the tents themselves.

Because all of my tent panels can open, the entrances are multiple. Visitors can wander right out onto the grass from wherever they are. This physical openness allows our minds to wander and open up to experiences that are unseen but deeply felt. Opening up to that multi-dimensional experience is part of our evolution as we pass through the paradigm shift.

When I walk from my bedroom tent into the dining tent, I feel connected to Mother Nature with every step. When it rains, I connect to her through the sound of the rain dripping from the edge of the canopy onto the leaves below. The soft breeze that wafts through my living spaces all day long makes me feel free. Amidst the abundance of nature, we no longer need to fear nature for our survival. Instead of caging ourselves away we can let her abundance come through. This is Living Without Walls.

258
259

Lighting is of utmost importance in these interior/exterior spaces. When all the panels are open, natural light fills the space. During a dark and rainy day, when there is no natural light, I strive to create an ambiance that inspires – rather than letting the darkness of the day bring down the mood. Even though the tents at The Sanctuary are aligned to sunrise and sunset, there are still days during the rainy season when, no matter where you are, it appears grey. For those days, I have installed energy-saving LED strips hidden behind the tented fabric ceilings. When I turn on the lights, I tell everybody who wants to hear that I am turning on the sun.

Biophilic city dwellers can create a pleasing environment by adding growing plants, green living walls, life-size nature posters and paintings, or by decorating with bare tree trunks. Through biophilic design, any urban space can be dressed up with the magic of nature. Whether we incorporate it in our homes or offices, it synchronizes us with the natural elements, keeping our body clocks in harmony.

When we bring nature indoors, it has been proven that it opens us up to a different state of awareness, one with which we are not so familiar. The experience relaxes us, dusts off stress, anxiety and negative thinking, promotes a happier state of being and a better night's sleep. Cumulatively these effects boost our immune systems, helping us to fight disease.

Large corporations such as Apple, Google and Amazon have successfully experimented with biophilic design. These companies have seen their teams become more motivated and have a more positive and happier outlook. Meandering through the building or garden paths boosts curiosity, while water features restore the body by reducing stress.

Even government departments have picked up on biophilic design. Coincidentally the same organization that brought Takashima Hokkai to France, the Japanese Ministry of Forestry, now promotes forest bathing (*shinrin-yoku*) to decrease chronic pain and depression, as well as encourage an appreciation of forest conservation.

Because more than half of the population lives in urban surroundings and spends more than 90% of their time indoors, we need to consider how to create harmony in these type of environments. It is a task for architects and designers to create spaces that have the comfort of being indoors while offering the same experience of well-being generated by life outdoors. We need to create spaces where children can learn happily and creatively, where workers will be both personally fulfilled and productive.

After a rampant period of coronavirus, we must once more establish a human connection with nature and its conservation. We need to fashion ourselves to this task, to deeply and fundamentally reconnect ourselves with the great outdoors. Biophilic design is a compelling, innovative and therapeutic way of designing the places in which we live, work and learn. It takes the concept of sustainability and our well-being to a new and deeper level, one in which we collaborate with nature's original creations. These creations can be delivered to us in the spaces we occupy by knowledgeable designers and architects.

Timeless Mindfulness, by William McDonough

"Modern life has come to embody what I call 'timeful mindlessness'. We are in a hurry and do not always respect the immediate impact of designs or their future effects on nature and humanity. However, Anneke's creation of elegant temporary structures is symbolic of moving toward a timeless mindfulness in which we think deeply about the things we make and the things we do. Her work is reminiscent of an essay I published nearly 20 years ago, *The Extravagant Gesture: Nature, Design, and the Transformation of Human Industry*, from which I share an excerpt:

"Nature is nothing if not extravagant. Four billion years of natural design, forged in the cradle of evolution, has yielded such a profusion of forms we can barely grasp the vigor and diversity of life on earth. Responding to unique local conditions, ants have evolved into nearly 10,000 species, several hundred of which can be found in the crown of a single Amazonian tree. Fruit trees produce thousands of blossoms – an astonishing abundance of blossoms – so that another tree might germinate, take root and grow. Birds too seem to have a taste for the extravagant: who could say the wood duck's plumage is restrained?

For most of our history, the human response to the living earth, to particular places, has expressed the same flowering of diversity. Bearing the uniquely human ability to imagine and create, we entered the show and developed our extravagant gestures. We built not just shelter, but beautiful, elegant responses to locale; the breathing, shade-providing Bedouin tent along with the ornate, aspiring temples of cool, coastal Japan. We designed not just wraps against the wind but tailored garments for ritual, celebration and our delight. We spoke and moved not just for utilitarian ends but to make drama and poetry, Balinese dance and Shakespearean verse – human creations stoking the fire.

Though human industry in the past 150 years has resorted to brute force rather than elegant design, commerce too could become a wellspring of creativity, productivity and pleasure. Think of the thriving marketplaces that have enlivened the world's great cities, the cherished objects and materials that transform shelter into a soulful dwelling. These need not be sacrificed to protect our forests, rivers, soil and air. Indeed, human industry and habitations can be designed to celebrate interdependence with other living systems, transforming the making and consumption of things into a regenerative force. Design can perform and preserve the extravagant gesture – in the marketplace, in the human community and in the natural world."

Sometimes I combine inspiration from nature with architectural influences to create surprising shapes. My Garden House was inspired by the Botanical Garden Pavilion in Brussels, as well as the body of a jellyfish. The shape gives the feeling of floating light as a feather, unbothered by the world below.

The Angel Oak, the largest live Southern Oak in the world. Photo by Philip Scalia.

Walnut Growth Table, by Mathias Bengtsson. Photo by Martin Krupp .

Tented Architecture for Global Nomads

Back in the early 1990s, environmental issues were of great concern to me. My aesthetic was informed by Wabi-Sabi simplicity, yet my lifestyle was anything but simple or naturalistic. I had sold a company and spent my time living the high life with the eccentric upper crust and bohemian artists who made up 'the scene'.

The big trigger for change was a single comment made by a friend I knew from my work with the United Nations. He said: "I don't understand why you're hanging out in these clubs and bars and going out to restaurants every single night. You could do something to change the world. You have that capacity." I thought, are you talking to me? Or is there someone standing behind me?

And that's when the penny dropped. I left everything, I packed up and decided to do something else. I turned off the whole thing. It was a beautiful life, I had a wonderful time, but somehow that one comment made me realize that my life was flat, that it would lead to nothing other than eventually becoming a retired socialite. I had so many interests and I realized that I had to leave New York if I wanted them to go anywhere. So I became a global nomad.

Continuing my Design for The Environment work, I took long trips throughout India, working with local conglomerates to improve factory conditions and explore alternative sustainable materials.

Because my travels throughout India often brought me to inhospitable locations with only very basic accommodation, I began to develop a travel kit of small luxuries to take with me. The kit included a high thread-count sleeping bag-style sheet that would make any bed I slept in comfortable; a nice portable mosquito net and all necessary toiletries I needed to bring comfort with me.

By 1999, my home base was a hotel suite on the beach in Bali. I decided to develop my kit into a product line, which I would display in a tent at my studio in Ubud. Naturally I started hosting gatherings, dinners, teas and small parties in my tent, and it grew to be a comfortable, well-lit space.

My hotel room featured the deep traditional wood couches common throughout Southeast Asia. I realized that two of these pieces could be put together, along with a long table that could be raised or lowered to form a multifunctional sitting, dining and sleeping space, all within four square meters. We still use this set in our designs today and the small multifunctional concept eventually grew into our Outpost tent.

At that time, I only had two tents: the display unit and a small portable 'floating tent', which I'd designed to take deep into nature.

One morning, coming back to Bali from an exhibition in India with the first tents I had designed I woke up inspired. I realized that I had found my vehicle. This flashpoint brought all of my previous ideas and influences together; I would design an even more luxurious tent, and I would live in it.

As I worked with local craftspeople to build the first unit, I immersed myself in the history of tents and tent interiors. My final designs were always pared down and understated, but the influence of these glamorous tent palaces of the past can still be seen.

"Humanity needs a vision of an expanding and unending future. This spiritual craving cannot be satisfied with the colonization of space. The true frontier for humanity is life on earth, its exploration and the transport of knowledge about it into science, art and practical affairs."

E.O. Wilson, Author of Biophilia [1]

This minimalist travel kit took me places and allowed me to feel comfortable in uncomfortable situations. I was able to bring five-star luxury with me wherever went. It had a net to ward off mosquitos, a fine cotton sleeping bag to keep out the crawlers, as well as soft padded slippers so I could land safely on unknown carpets.

40,000 BC Mammoth Tent made of Skin Tusks and Bones
Tent ruins have been found in Russia dating back as far as 40.000 BC when mammoths were still roaming our planet.

After living in caves, homo sapiens gave birth to tents.

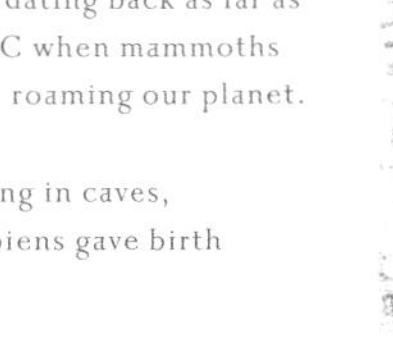

1400 BC
The portable sanctuary
In the Hebrew Bible, the Jewish tribes constructed a tented shrine as their place of worship. Their God is a Nomad's God.

600 BC
Herodotus described Scythians living in yurts,
which are still used to this day throughout Central and North Asia. The mobility of the construction allowed these nomad groups to spread throughout the world, creating vibrant and diverse cultures, customs, mythologies and philosophies.

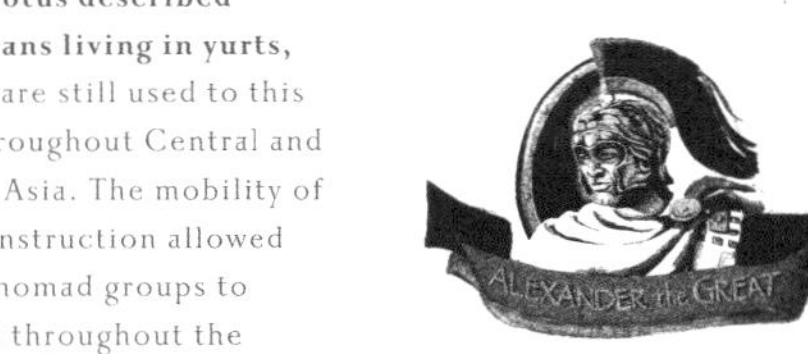

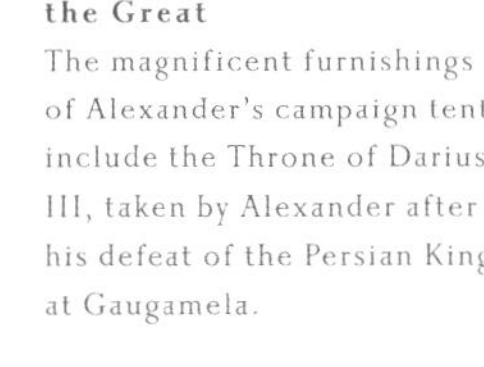

350 – 323 BC Alexander the Great
The magnificent furnishings of Alexander's campaign tent include the Throne of Darius III, taken by Alexander after his defeat of the Persian King at Gaugamela.

100-44 BC Julius Caesar Roman Empire tent
The tents of the all-conquering Roman legions were made from goat and/or calfskin.

1299 CE, ended in 1922 Ottoman Empire
The Movable Tent Cities of the Ottoman Empire
The most lavish among them were festooned with colorful appliqué and brightened with gilded leather.

Ottoman Empire Sultan Ahmed Khan.

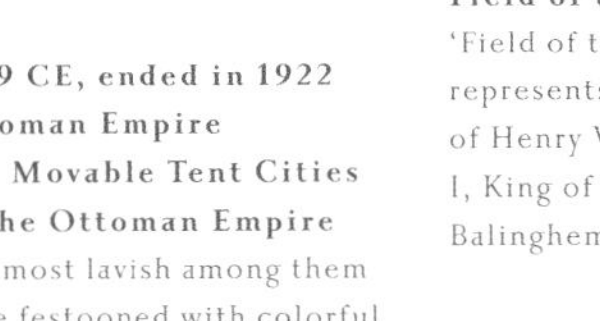

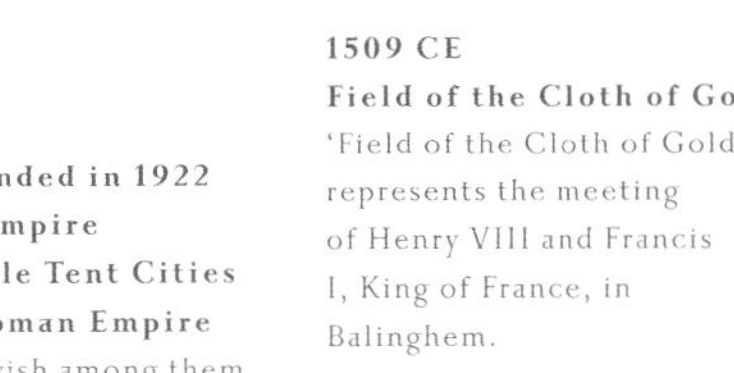

Henry VII

1509 CE
Field of the Cloth of Gold
'Field of the Cloth of Gold' represents the meeting of Henry VIII and Francis I, King of France, in Balinghem.

1556-1605 CE
Mughal Kings Tents
The Mughal Emperor Akbar is said to have lavishly patronized art during his era. His style was a mixture of Persian and Indian motifs, which was reflected in the magnificent tents, carpets, and furniture captured by the Ottoman army in the seventeenth century.

1700 CE Tipis
Following the arrival of the horse to North America, the Lakota people abandoned their sedentary lifestyle and became nomads on the planes, living in their formerly seasonal portable dwelling, the tipi. Their mobile lifestyle allowed them to become some of the most skilled warriors in the continent

1807 Meeting of Emperors. Alexander of Russia and Napoleon Bonaparte of France at the Neman near Tilsit on July 1807. Tents were used on official state visits, conquests and trading missions. Later, European royalty would use tents for elaborate outdoor festivals, hunting trips and season-long garden parties.

1900 Safari Tents
A wall tent also known as an outfitter tent, safari tent, or sheep herder tent, is a type that has four straight vertical walls providing more headroom than traditional pyramid-shaped varieties. Wall tents are typically made of a heavy canvas and are used by hunters ... as they are able to accommodate a wood stove. In recent years, they have also become popular for glamping.

2015 Glamping tents
The portmanteau of 'glamorous' and 'camping became popular with 21st-century escapists and adventure seekers as an alternative to camping.

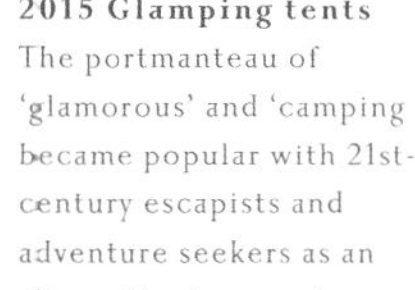

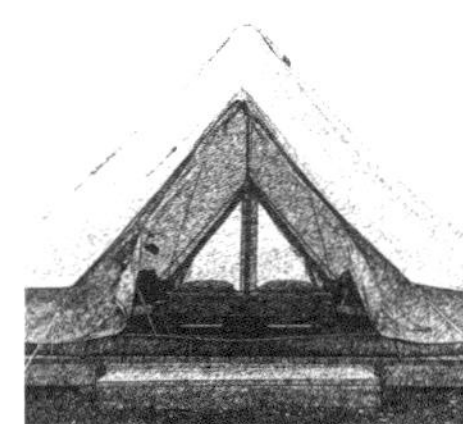

2005 Escape Nomade Haute Couture Architecture tents.
Less rustic tents with full private staff are semi-permanent with heavy-duty metal framework. Made for the hospitality industry to use as a bedroom, spa, restaurant, rooftop or pool covering. Royal tents and private residences are made from high-quality nano technology fabrics that last a lifetime.

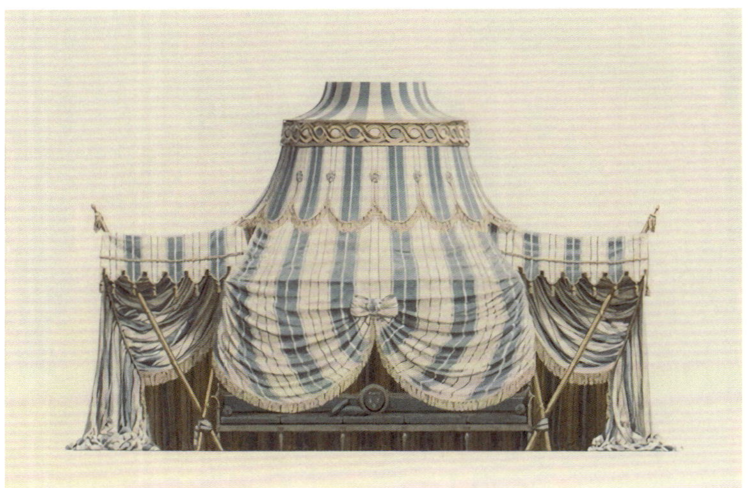

Images from left to right, top to bottom: *The Turkish Tent in the Parc Monceau, Paris* by Edward Andrew Zega. *Equestrian Portrait of Guidoriccio da Fogliano*, by Simone Martini. *The tent-room in Charlottenhoff Palace*, by Karl Friedrich Schinkel. Striped silk robe a la Francaise, photographed by Kerry Taylor Auctions. Striped silk robe a la Francaise, photographed by Kerry Taylor Auctions. *Meeting of Emperors Alexander I of Russia and Napoleon I of France at the Neman Near Tilsit*, by Jean Baptiste Debret. *Dressing the Landscape*, by Barbara-Issa Wagner.

Once upon a time the majority of humanity lived in temporary structures. As most humans became settled in permanent habitations, tents continued to be used on the battlefield. Generals and kings held sway in jeweled canvas palaces. Now kings, sultans, rajas and khans enthroned themselves in nature. From these tented thrones they conquered territories and negotiated treaties, dividing the spoils of the subdued earth.

Most tents in the 18th and 19th centuries were made of duck cloth, linen made from cotton or hemp. One of the problems with this material was that when packed the fabrics tended to decay. The development of nylon and similar fabrics has put an end to duck cloth. Insulation has become possible thanks to the lessons learned by tent manufacturers during the World Wars, which included fighting in cold terrain and wet areas. Finally, tent shapes went from a basic canvas-thrown-over-sticks style to include much more structured designs. Most tents were made from a fabric consisting of a knitted high-tenacity PVC coated vinyl prime, with a protective Teflon treatment. Hardly healthy.

Our Haute Couture tents are made with the highest quality nanotechnology techniques to invent fabrics that prevent the dangers of leakage or mildew and last a long time. At Escape Nomade, once our roof fabrics reach the end of their life cycle, we give them to artists and make gift bags for holiday celebrations at the company.

Any tent made 100% with natural material cannot resist the weather conditions to keep the fabrics long-lasting and functional. Luckily most Escape Nomade accessories and fabric suppliers respect the environment at heart. Sunbrella, our fabric supplier, prohibits the highly polluting stages normally used in the weaving process. Their fabric treatment is optimized to avoid overloading products with chemicals. The stiffening product they use, for example, also has a double function and guards against decay. Treatment processes are carried out in a closed circuit. The solution-dyeing of their yarns guarantees color-fastness and saves water. It allows them to avoid the use of conventional dyes, which pollute and consume water. The small volume of water used in their weaving process is fully recycled in-house. The Green Ovation approach takes end-of-life into account for all products. Selvage yarns are partly recycled to produce industrial filters, insulation products and outdoor rugs. All waste from their head office and production site is fully organized. Some 300 metric tons of waste is sorted each year for specific recycling and used for new product ranges, like their Replay range, which contains 30% recycled material.

We work together with our suppliers to consider and adopt the use of materials. We consider the earth's fragility, an essential principle of Haute Couture Architecture.

Like a raindrop beading up on a lotus leaf, spherical droplets on the nanofiber Sunbrella tent fabric I use roll smoothly over the surface. Along the way, they pick up dirt, dust and other contaminants, carrying them away and cleaning the fabric. This is due to the pencil-like, conical design of the nanostructures within the fabric, trapping air and ensuring only a tiny amount of water contacts the surface. This property of super-hydrophobia is found in the lotus, as well as 300 other plant species. Insects such as dragonflies and butterflies have this same property on the surface of their wings. By learning from processes in nature, the fabric is able to naturally protect itself from water, dirt and mildew.

We use another well-known product that is also a great example of design inspired by nature: the humble and versatile Velcro. Swiss engineer George de Mestral invented Velcro in 1941 after he removed burrs from his dog and decided to take a closer look at how they worked. The small hooks found at the end of the burr needles inspired him to create the now omnipresent Velcro. We use it to attach the wall panels and pole covers, which are never seen but highly useful. Without this material, the installation of Escape Nomade tented compositions would have been much more complicated. It allows us to use lighter materials and makes it easy for anyone to open and close a wall panel.

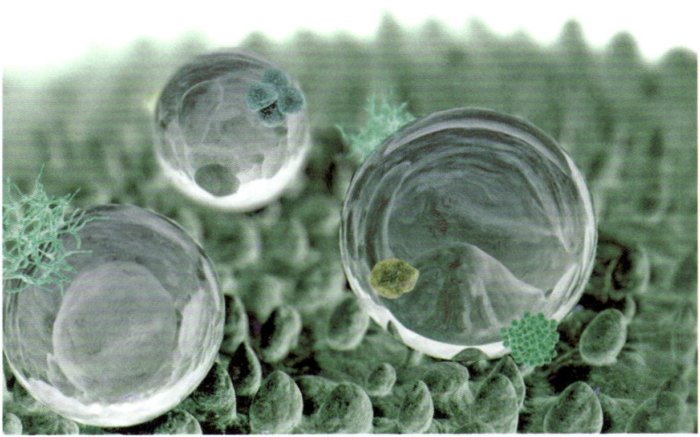

Rain water and dirt roll off the tent roof fabric in a similar way to water on a lotus leaf. This is what we call 'biomimicry', the study of how we can apply natural processes to sustainable products.

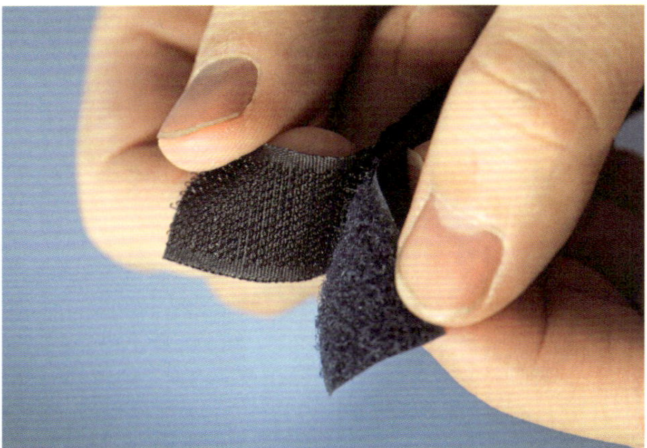

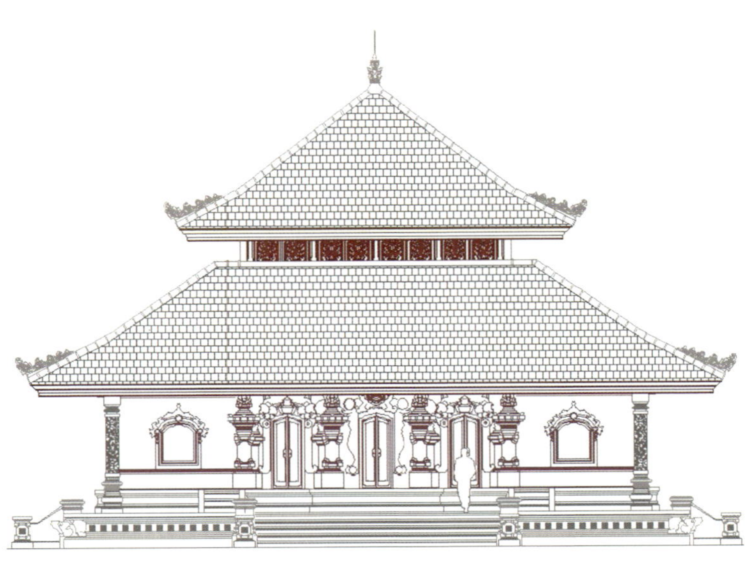

Balinese Vernacular Architecture

Spend enough time in Bali and it is impossible not to notice the ubiquitous double-roofed *wantilan* design used for many traditional buildings. These structures are used for private and public spaces, cultural events and other general uses.

The double roof design allows for simple natural ventilation. Rolling bamboo screens instead of fixed walls allow for multiple uses of the interior space. These multifunctional and energy-saving designs were an obvious match with my thinking and were incorporated into my design improvements. We have gone further, adding small roll-up windows, flexible insulation within the wall panels and even a courtyard style unit where the second roof is removed completely.

Balinese buildings are constructed with attention to the human and spiritual landscape that surrounds them. While our tents use standardized measurements, the tent sizes and their placement within the landscape reflect real human needs. Bigger is not always better.

Traditional tools for building a house or a temple in Bali. On the day of *tempak jandap*, a holiday designated in the Balinese calendar for the blessing of all metals, these tools are charged by a priest.

Our team and the priest blessing The Sanctuary's metal building tools, car, bicycle, and tent frames.

When building a house, the Balinese measure distances based on the size of the owner's body, and in the case of a public building, the size of the head of the village.

Balinese Units of Measurement

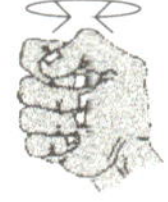

Agamel

Size of the fist. Units are the number of fists placed on top of each other.

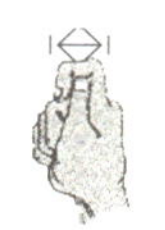

Aguli

Thickness of the pointer finger when hooked over the thumb.

Alek

Length of the middle finger.

Akacing

Length of the pinky.

Amusti

Length from thumb to pinky in a closed hand.

Duang Nyari

Width of pointer and middle finger.

Tampak Lima

Width of palm.

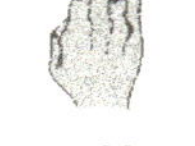

Pegang Nyari

Width of knuckles.

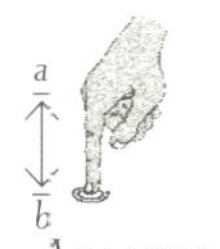

Auseran

Length of pointer finger.

Acengkang

Length from extended tip of thumb to extended tip of pointer finger.

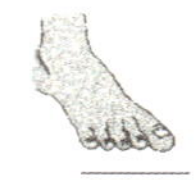

Atapak Betis Ngandang

Width of all toes.

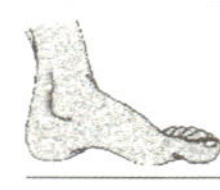

Atapak Betis

Length of foot.

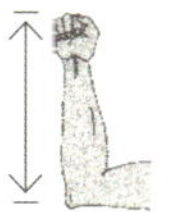

Sahasta

Width of forearm.

Atengan Depa Alit

Length of arm with fist closed.

Atengan Depa Agung

Length of arm with fingers open.

Adepa

Length of outstretched arms from fingertip to fingertip.

In Balinese culture, months of the year are considered to metaphorically represent the cycle of human life. The first nine months represent the period of pregnancy before birth, the tenth month represents the birth of the human into the world, the eleventh month the end of his or her existence, the twelfth month is the return to where he or she came from.

As the cycle goes from one spark of conception to another, it traverses through the void: *suwung*.

The concept of *suwung* is originally from Javanese and describes a state of consciousness in which one produces no mental forms (thoughts) but is fully self-aware and aware of the environment. It is thought of as a state of grace.

Suwung is also seen as the origin of the universe, an original essence, an absolute reality that cannot be reached by the human senses. In the Hindu-Buddhist philosophies of ancient Java and Bali, pure awareness stems from this pregnant void that is neither temporal nor non-temporal.

This transcendent philosophy is also inherent in the aesthetic of solitude and desolation expressed through Wabi-Sabi. By celebrating fleeting beauty it points to the invisible source and destination of all matter and experience.

In the Western world, the idea of an unseen reality, underlying that which is seen, suggests an unknowable creator who lays beyond our limited lives.

To worship this unseen creator, the ancient Hebrews draped the natural landscape in a tabernacle of cloth. Similarly, the Arabs covered a rock that had fallen from the heavens in black cloth, framed by holy mountains and sacred wells. With these creations of holy cloth, they worshipped an invisible god, an unknown and unknowable force that created the natural world. They placed humanity within it as the protector, master and shepherd.

These temporary cloth thrones implicitly reject the idea that our creations should be permanent, yet they are a refinement of the human ideal. Like a Balinese temple, the structures themselves represent cosmic harmony and balance.

All of us have the ability to achieve this harmony and balance by accessing the unseen in our own ways. We can express our experience with the unseen and point others towards it through our actions. We can participate in creation by designing our lives and the world in which we dream to live in. We pull the golden thread through the eye of the needle, weaving a better world for the future.

We can participate in creation by designing our lives and the world in which we dream to live in.

The Hebrews created a tabernacle of perishable human-made cloth, a stark but temporary beacon draping the landscape.

VII.
Haute Couture Architecture

"Ripples sent out through the fabric of space & time"

Living Without Walls

Living Outside the Box

Living With Intent

Haute Couture Architecture bridges the gap between architecture and nature. It gently drapes and dresses the void.

It embodies humanity within the divine environment, born to show the emergencies that we face and to awaken humanity to a new paradigm.

I realize that Haute Couture Architecture might sound at first like an oxymoron; I adopted the idea to evoke the pre-modern sense of high luxury that values quality materials and craftsmanship. 'Haute Couture' is most commonly used to imply high-end compositions made from superior quality fabrics, sewn with close attention to detail and finished by the hands of experienced couturiers. The sewing process for my tents is similar, and they are tailored specifically for individuals. The accessories accompanying an Haute Couture garment are hand-made and applied, similar to the way the belts and bamboo pole covers that grace our tents are hand-fitted.

When I develop new designs I work as a couturier but on a large scale. I climb staircases next to the tents with measuring tape around my neck, needle, thread and scissors on hand to check the fitting. The feeling comes off in the stitching, the textures, the proportions. Form should always follow function, just as in a luxury car, a Swiss watch or a designer dress. Our artisanal tailored spaces are intended to be as evocative of an elegant, alluring, imaged past as they are accessible to the needs of a living being.

Architecture and haute couture design have a culture of aesthetics in common. Both protect us from the elements and are the sanctuaries for our human bodies. Pliable, lightweight glass and other flexible building materials are now illuminating the catwalks while climate-controlled 'wearable habitats' give shelter to our bodily sanctuaries.

Designers and architects alike are inspired by the pleats of Fortuny and Issey Miyake or the buildings of Zaha Hadid. Through textures, shapes, and forms in space and time, architects and designers inform one another and transform lives into new creations. Haute couture dresses bodies with wearable art, while architecture dresses the places in which we work and live. On the interrelation between fashion and architecture, Coco Chanel said: "Fashion is architecture, it is a matter of proportions."

Pierre Balmain, Gianfranco Ferré, Fernando Garcia, Versace, Coco Chanel, Pierre Cardin ... all had an architectural background. Some of them studied architecture and switched to fashion. Cardin studied architecture in Paris. Influenced by his background in architectural study, he was known for his inclination towards applying geometrical shapes and motifs in his fashion design. Haute couture and architecture have a long-lasting relationship.

Our vision is to steer this muse in a new direction. Design can be influenced by anything. Haute Couture Architecture is driven by nature to focus its shape, its functions and its simplicity. Like haute couture in fashion, our constructions are not stagnant. They have movement and are impermanent. My buildings communicate with the seasons, with time and space.

While I use techniques similar to those of high luxury, what inspired me initially was an observance of nature and conservation, provoking new dialogues with sustainability. I work to reimagine the concept of luxury by celebrating simplicity, the sacred and sustainability.

Haute Couture Architecture is about re-creating a sense of belonging to the natural world, transcending the present and returning to that treasured past when the earth was still heaven. The physical footprint and environmental impact of my tents should be flawless.

A couturier can use an unusual covering to morph the human body, making the model appear as if she grew from nature. In my buildings, I clad Mother Nature herself in our cloth, uplifting and offering respect.

PM
LIVING

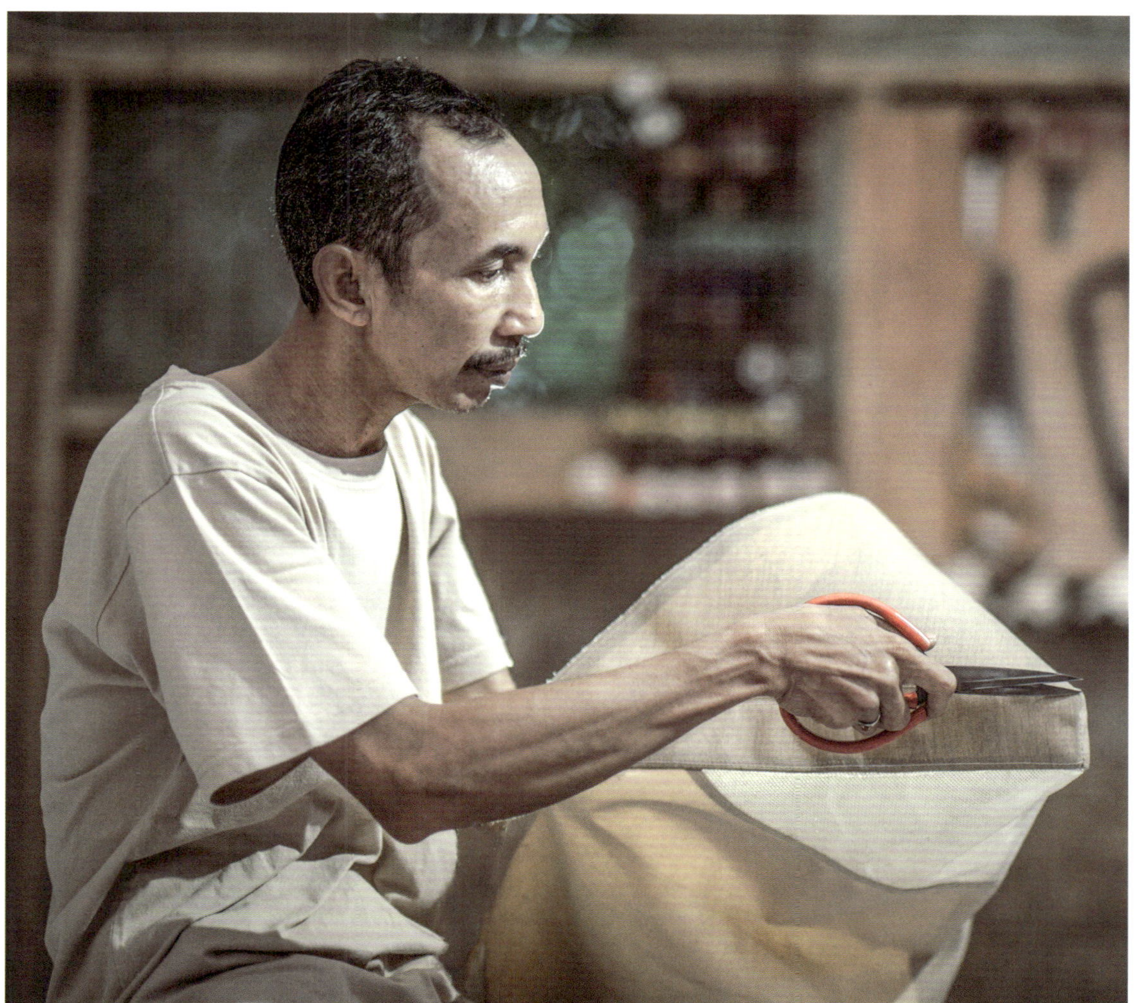

I strive to articulate the opposite of that aesthetic of excess often disguised as luxury.

Excess draws from the suppressed fear of never having enough. Because of our historical past, this fear is in our DNA. But that built-in fear of oppression and of not having enough is waging war against the environment and the very planet we live on.

We cannot compare our lives with that of royalties who lived extravagantly in the past. The new upper and middle classes that followed them wanted the same, and it has led to the catastrophes and calamities we are facing today.

We never have enough possessions, but we can't ever get enough love, power and attention either. These substitutes for emptiness are the top priority drivers destroying this world of plenty. Even though nature is fighting back, she still shows her abundance by displaying extravagance to those who open their eyes to it.

The luxury of simplicity embodied within Haute Couture Architecture is very different from typical architectural minimalism. Minimalist architecture tends to be industrial and precise, with no space for emotion.

On the contrary, Haute Couture Architecture understands that less is more. It inspires to honor imperfection. It allows deep emotion, ultimate freedom, heartfelt empathy and abundance with gratitude.

> *"You can mould clay into a vessel; yet, it is its emptiness that makes it useful."*
>
> Lao Tzu

When stepping on Mother Nature's soil to build, we unintentionally step onto her soul – the soul to which we are all connected.

Haute Couture Architecture questions the consequences of construction. It questions what a location can support within its natural environment, fauna and flora.

My creations should look as if they were lightly dropped amidst nature and could easily be carried away. As if they only existed in a dream. However, the unseen reality is that beneath those soft, ephemeral canvas shapes lays a steel structure capable of withstanding even heavy winds. The cladding cleverly conceals their strength, while the fabric softly displays a fragility. Within it is the shadow of the invisible footprint that we don't leave behind.

With Haute Couture Architecture, we seek to strip away the residue of wasteful materials and outmoded ways of building and thinking. We start from the ground up by engaging basic human needs: a bedroom, bathroom, living room, kitchen, a floor, a natural landscape. It is not just these elements, however, that make a home. It is the void between them that creates a habitat where human beings can live consciously, finding balance and harmony with nature.

This philosophy means knowing you are living in a void and taking up nature's space. It inspires us to be grateful and to tread lightly.

I strive to build new relationships with the physical space around me by transmitting the message I receive from the soul of Mother Nature, as it is whispered directly into my heart. I ask permission from the sacred space to fashion its natural landscape to my vision. I seek to honor nature's attention to every detail in my designs and with my team's craft. Like everything in nature that flows, my creations are transformed and merged into the depth of her landscapes.

When I design, I start from simplicity, go into intricate complexity, and back to simplicity. It is a living example of holding back excess and staying with the essentials. What I reach is a liveable-space design made of pure materials and simple shapes.

As I envision it, Haute Couture Architecture is based on the relationship between humans and the divine, humans with one another and humans with nature. It makes sense that the philosophy of 'taking up nature's space' and asking her permission inspires us to be grateful.

My creations should look as if they were lightly dropped amidst nature.

> *"There is more to life than increasing its speed."*
>
> Mahatma Gandhi

While I am certainly a designer of luxury tents, I find the concept that is typically described by the word 'glamping' to be the antithesis of what I do. Row upon row of cheaply made tents adorning a lifeless field, constructed of components that must be replaced every two years, displays a lack of thinking about the calamity caused to the environment. Haute Couture Architecture is about sanctifying and uplifting both nature and humanity, not about transferring the industrial world to a glamorous camping ground. We don't need to create a suburb of tents in a field in order to hit a specific price point (as they used to say in the old paradigm). A more careful and subtler forethought doesn't cost a thing. Cheap production and the urge to make things affordable for everyone has until now been at the cost of our precious environment.

The pandemic emergency facing us I believe highlights the need to awaken humanity to the New Paradigm. By acting for the general good, we will celebrate nature's lasting beauty again, as we did for so many generations.

I express this through my designs by building a new relationship with physical space and creating a sense of belonging that harks back to a time when the earth was still heaven.

Haute Couture Architecture is a product of its time. To prevent the disastrous implications of our short-sighted decisions in an often paralyzed world, I use design to acknowledge the urgency of change. Architects and designers play an important role in diverting us from the road that leads to the destruction of our remaining pristine landscapes, and we must live outside the box and adopt a fearless approach. It should come across as a call from close to nature, whispered directly into the heart, inspiring within us a new dream for humanity.

I strive to create friendly abodes in which people will like to dwell for the rest of their lives. An abode from which to celebrate the wonders and the beauty of nature. A place where we feel a sense of belonging informed by living spirits, transformed by our human involvement and imagination.

I design for a purpose – to fulfill the client's dream with heart and soul. With these tents, we can go to places nobody else can go, and we can do it in cozy comfort. Each breath taken in a forest, every silent moment on a mountain top watching the same sunrise our ancestors once watched connects us to our true nature. The complexity of simplicity made us who we are both as individuals and collectively as one living, breathing human race.

My interior designs highlight the natural patterns of unadorned material. They feature few material possessions, no attachments, just a small number of curated items with a history. These atmospheres rebuild the connection between humans and nature that existed for thousands of years, back when all of our homes were caves, huts or tents. At my Sanctuary, I can surrender to nature's tranquility for relief and relaxation. It improves my happiness factor by 100%.

There should seemingly be no difference between inside and outside in Haute Couture Architecture. As we lay back on couches for tea and discussion, butterflies flit in and out, bird song reaches us from the garden, and a gentle breeze cools our skin.

Human culture started when we first heard a noise in the forest and imagined what lay behind it. Storytelling and sharing those experiences of the unseen world shaped who we are.

Lying on our backs, watching the clouds pass by, our senses are tuned to perceive recognizable shapes, patterns, animals, faces or objects. As we continue to watch, those images change; rabbits morph into ducks, the face of a young woman changes into that of an older adult. At moments like this, we leave our everyday consciousness and go into the cosmic realm, daydreaming and bathing in its blurry substance.

“Be that pioneer to whole new continents and worlds within you, opening new channels, not of trade, but of thought.”

Henry David Thoreau

Haute Couture Architecture is very much about expressing the romance of travel and the longing that goes with it – the longing for more spirituality, individuality and space.

At one time in my life, I always had an airline ticket in my pocket. If somebody asked me where I lived, I could not always give a direct answer. At that time, living in one place was unknown to me and to most people I knew. A lucky few have always had the ability to live as international citizens with no permanent residence, or perhaps several in different countries. Though they may return to their homeland from time to time, their version of Living Without Walls is to be free from their homeland 's society. Fast forward thirty-five years and technology has made it possible for many professionals to work from anywhere, creating a new tribe of digital nomads. The lockdown of 2020 has proven that it can be done. At home or in the foothills of the Himalayas, business and pleasure can now be always at hand. Whether they have the means to live globally as a lifestyle choice, or travel the world while working remotely, I think of this new culture collectively as the Global Nomads. These ‘glomads’ create and spread the seed of new ways of living across the globe. If unknown developments do not occur to destroy international travel as we know it, there is no doubt that the way of glomadic life will grow more popular.

Today, though, I have become more of a ‘homead’. Now I live permanently in Bali with few possessions, no other residences or responsibilities, and I have never been happier. The feeling of having roots and living a stable life gives shape to my ideas and experiences. My nomadic spirit is now rooted, bringing inner freedom, flexibility and appreciation of nature as I settle under her open skies.

Ultimately, Haute Couture Architecture gives a new direction to the world-weary. Those who desire to explore, to pioneer, and to seek inspiration. It is a portal to alternative thinking.

To live close to nature within tents with no secrets, no valuable possessions and no fear of losing anything gives me a sense of revolutionary euphoria. I feel far away from the mundane materialistic world that has stressed us out and messed us up. This way of life does not conceal but reveals; no hidden secrets, no entrapments, no doors that can be slammed. It is a vision of being a free human with gratitude, simplicity and the luxury of discovering that all good things in life are free. This feeling of freedom gives me a way to enter the space and wisdom of the good spirits who dwelled on earth long before we arrived.

We have been taught to think that we can only stay comfortable by locking ourselves in a hermetically sealed box, controlling the experience inside by cutting off the world outside. Haute Couture Architecture is instead about artfully working with nature. It is meant to make us feel fully in nature and fully human, lifted, glorified, free and without worry. The fully aware human is both experiencer and experience, consciousness through the eye of the needle. It is that needle we use in our creations, the empty space of the eye filled with a golden thread that ties together the visible and the invisible.

It is time to open up and live outside the box.

Ex Libris

Non Nobis Solum - 'Not for us but for everyone'.

The Tree of Life, a colossal interwoven 'worldwide web' of unlimited energy above and below us, unites our limited 'me' into a more significant 'we', and indeed into a more prominent 'you'. We are connected cosmic creatures.

As we learn and grow, the Tree of Life becomes the Tree of Knowledge. Novel neuroscience reveals that the mysterious source of life lies in our connection with energies that we have only just discovered.

Our natural birthright is to connect the heavens and the earth through our deep roots and tall branches. What unique beings we are, for inside of every one of us hides the entire cosmos.

The new paradigm thinking from 'me' only, to 'we' together.

The End

Haute Couture Architecture

Photographers:

A

De Agostini, tent-room in Charlottenhof Palace 270

Angel House Ubud 36

Dzianis Apolka, Alamy 127

Sergey Aleluhin, Vitebsk railway station in St. Petersburg 218

Gerd Altmann, Pixabay 76

Ansonsaw, istockphoto, sprouting seedling 66

Hike Arijs, Cauchie House, Brussels 222

Stephane Bahler, Raffles Hotel, Siem Reap 189

B

Bali Wedding Guide 43

Robert Balog, Pixabay, kingfisher 41

Djuna Bewley, tents at Escape Nomade Sanctuary, Bali 57, 58, 258, 279, 283, 291

Karl Blossfeldt, black and white macro close-ups of plants and living things 223, 224

David Brooke Martin, Jade plant cutting in water, Unsplash 230

Eveline de Bruin, La Gabarra factory in La Bisbal d'Empordà, Catalonia 219

Emily Burbank, Fortuny dress worn by Mrs. Condé Nast 222

C

Santi Caleca, Hermes Tent Pavilion 245, 246, 247

Jeanne Claude Christo, Running Fence, Sonoma and Marin Counties, CA 249, 250, 251

D

Jean- Pierre Dabera, Art Nouveau Furniture by Horta, CC 227

Danderot, Kintsugi, Mishima Ware 236

Dalyong, Pixabay, morning dew 67

Don Davidon, Spider web with dew 282

Tinjana Drndarski, Unsplash, candle 103

Rob Dun, Swirling growth from a melon vine plant 225

E

Gabby Eidt, wehearit, autumn fairy 62

Edo Emmerig, Pixabay, coconuts 102

Camilla Engman, Art Nouveau gate, Gothenburg, Sweden 219

F

Johnathon Fortino, Palm House Botanic Garden, Schönbrunn, Austria 264

G

Yvette Gauthier, Flower-shop, Brussels 219

Isabella Gianneschi 5

Photo Courtesy of ©RMN-Grand Palais, musée d'Orsay/Hervé, vases by Emile Gallé 226

H

Katherine Hanlon, Unsplash, mortar and pestle 103

Christine Hume, Unsplash, essential oil 89

I

Villy Fink Isaksen, Commons Wikimedia, zesting a lime 51

J

Jastrow. J, Rabbit and duck illusion, CC 112

K

Kira Auf Der Heide, Unsplash, person holding crystal stones 89

Mikolaj Krawczunas, Saatschi Art 55, 97, 116, 146, 289

Martin Krupp, Walnut Growth Table by Mathias Bengtsson 265

Joana Kruse, Pura Besakih, Bali 251

Kura Kura, Bali 194, 195, 196, 197

L

Robert Landau, Art Deco apartment façade, Brussels 223

Tafline Laylin, the root bridge in Meghalaya, India, CC 7

Christopher Little, Falling Water, Frank Lloyd Wright 248

M

Anne Sophie Maestracci, drone over Kapuhala 179

Kayla Maurais, Burning sage, Unsplash 88

Sharon McCutcheon, merging hands, Unsplash 109

Mark McKim, group of tents left, Kapuhala Resort 278

Hannah Gabrielle More @ Aarunya Resort Kandy Sri Lanka 176

Raphael Moriniere, Sanctuary tents, Bali, Indonesia 17, 27, 29

Mossmessiah @ Aarunya Resort Kandy Sri Lanka 172, 174

Myriam, Sparkler Lightbulb, Pixabay 67

N

Zai Nomura, Watercolor, The Beige, Camboadia 150

O

Roman Odintsov, Aarunya Resort Kandy Sri Lanka 176

P

Luca Piazzi, picnic 86, 212

Martin Puddy 7, 8, 9, 10, 11 (tents), 120,123, 124, 125, 128, (right), 129, (right), 130, 132, 134, 138, 140, 143, (right), 144 (top), 145, 148, 151, 152, (bottom), 153, 154, 155, 156, 157, 158, 159, 160, 161, 162, 163, 165, 166, 167, 169, 170, 178, 179 (right&bottom). 182 (right). 186, 187, 215, 261, 263, 273, 274 (right), 276, 284, 285, 290.

Primimpil, iStock, Head with light 67

Cristian Prisecariu, purple dew drops, Pixabay 66

Q

R

Nath Rankothge & Associates 171, 172, 173 174, 175, 176

S

Ivaras Sarapovas, Kapuhala Resort, Koh Samui 180, 183, 185

Philip Scalia, the Angel Oak, Charleston, SC 265

Jillian Schleger, Piabay, nature-bee-bumblebee-flight-flower 67

Courtesy of Selong Selo 190, 191

Kuòān Shīyuǎn, Wikipedia, ten bulls 70

Silviarita, Pixabay rosebud dewdrop of water 67

Yaeko Simmonds 80, 144 (bottom), 208

Courtesy of Sotheby's Est. with Auguste and Antonin Daum 1744, design by Louis Majorelle "magnolia" three-light table lamp 230

Shin Sugino 242, 243, 244

Yano Sumampow, Imagine 46, 47, 260

T

Henry Townsend, Victor Horta, Staircase Hotel Tassel 221

Keiichi Tahara, Maison et Atelier Horta 220

Sasin Tipchai, Pixabay, Asian Boys 33, 36, 41

U

Giezi Uzziel, Pixabay, shadow tree black and white

V

Wolfgang Volz, The Gates by Christo and Jeanne-Claude, Central Park, NY 251

W

Anneke van Waesberghe 40, 43, 44, 49, 51, 52, 53, 54, 55 (right), 87, 88, 90, 93, 95, 96, 99 (right) 100, 101, 102, 103(left), 104, 105, 106, 118, 131, 143 (left), 199. 200, 201, 204, 243, 235 (left), 236, (left/ right), 237, 238, 239, 240, 256, 267, 280

Y

Tanaka Yohu, Fish Design 225

Donald Young, Newland, Tarlton Safaris 13

Z

Ruslan Zh, Unsplash 66

Artists:

Edmond Auguin, Portrait Takashima Hokkai 226

Christo and Jeanne Claude, Running Fence, Sonoma and Marin Counties, CA, 1976, USA 249, 250, 251

Tatiana Efimova, Watercolors, 2020, Bali, Indonesia 4, 28, 30, 32, 56, 59, 69, 75, 84, 110, 115, 122, 135, 136, 137, 149, 202, 217, 255, 296

George Dionysius Ehret, Trew, C.J, (1750-73), Illustration flowering fig tree leaves, UK 231

Kesai Eisen, Courtesan, Courtesy of van Gogh Museum, Amsterdam, The Netherlands 232

Gustav Klimt, Hope II, Courtesy of Museum of Modern Art, New York 233

Meyers Konversations – Lexikon, Four of the most important domesticated silk moths, (1839-1984), Germany, CC 218

Otto Wilhelm Thome, illustration Narcissus poeticus and myrtus,1895, Cologne, Germany 231

Vincent Van Gogh, Blooming Plum, 1887, Courtesy van Gogh Museum, Amsterdam, The Netherlands 230

Vincent Van Gogh, Portrait of Père Tanguy, 1887, Courtesy van Gogh Museum, Amsterdam, The Netherlands 232

Haute Couture Architecture Influences:

René Wiener, Japanese print on wood, Nancy, France 233. left

Barbara-Issa Wagner, 2019, Dressing the landscape, Czech Republic 271 right bottom

Designers:

Mathias Bengtsson,Walnut Growth Table, 2014, Copenhagen, Denmark 265

Pierre Cardin, Bubble Dress, 1995, Paris, France 281

Emile Gallé, Model of the four sides of two earthenware vases, 1885, Nancy, France 226

Louis Majorelle "Magnolia", three-light table lamp,1903, France 230

Anak Agung Gede Sudarma Putra Pemayun, Escape Nomade, 2018, Bali, Indonesia 188

Striped silk robe à la Francaise, 18th Century, Courtesy of Taylor auctions, London, UK 270

Karl Friedrich Schinkel, tent-room in Charlottenhof Palace, 1805, Potsdam, Germany 270

Angga Wiyana, Escape Nomade, 2019, Bali, Indonesia Book Cover

Phillipe Wolfers, Dragonfly, 1902/03, Brussels, Belgium 226

Architects:

Shigeru Ban, the Hermes Pavilion, 2011, Paris, France 245, 246, 247

Escape Nomade, 2010-2020, Bali, Indonesia cover, 5, 6, 7, 8, 9, 10, 11, 27, 39, 45, 48, 52, 57, 58, 74, 81, 82, 123, 124, 125, 128, 129, 130, 138, 144, 146, 148, 151, 153, 154, 156, 162, 166, 167, 169, 170, 171, 176, 177, 178, 179, 186, 187, 188, 189, 190, 192, 193, 194, 195, 197, 205, 208, 209, 215, 258, 259, 260, 273, 274, 278, 279, 284, 285, 287, 288, 290, 291, 294

Paul Gauchie, Private House, 1905, Brussels, Belgium, CC 223

Paul Hankar, Flower shop, former Maison Niguet, 1896, Rue Royale, Brussels, Belgium, CC 219

Victor Horta, Maison & Atelier, skylight and mirror, 1898, Brussels, Belgium, CC 220

Victor Horta, Staircase Hotel Tassel, 1892/93, Brussels, Belgium, CC 221

Sima Mihash and Stanislav Brzozowski, Whiplash Motifs at Vityebsky railway station, 1904, St Petersburg, Russia CC 218 Left

Gustav Strauven, Art Deco apartment façade, 1903, Brussels, Belgium CC 223

Kingo Tatsuno, house of Matsumoto Kenjito, 1911, Kitakiyushu, Japan 228

Henry van de Velde, The Bloemenwerf, 1895, Brussels, Belgium 228

Frank Lloyd Wright, Falling Water, 1935, Fayette County, Pennsylvania, USA, 248

Reference

Audio:

I. *The Serviceberry: An Economy of Abundance,* By Robert Wall Kimmerer
https://emergencemagazine.org/story/the-serviceberry/

Movies:

I. *HUMAN,* A film by Yann Arthus-Bertrand, music composed by Armand Amar
http://www.human-themovie.org/

II. *Aluna,* A film by Alan Ereira, with the Kogi tribe
http://alunathemovie.com/find

Video:

I. The channel of Dr. Joe Dispenza
https://www.youtube.com/user/drjoedispenza

II. *Biology of Belief,* the channel of Dr. Bruce Lipon Ph.D.
https://www.youtube.com/user/biologyofbelief

III. *Gregg Braden Official,* the channel of Gregg Braden
https://www.youtube.com/user/

Books:

I. *The Seven Spiritual Laws of Success,* by Deepak Chopra

II. *The Longing For Less,* by Kyle Chayka

III. *Lotek: Design by Radical Indigenism,* by Julia Watson

IV. *Silent Spring,* Rachel Carson

V. *East Meets West in Design: Archaeology of the Present,* by Anneke van Waesberghe

VI. *Skin + Bones: Parallel Practices in Fashion and Architecture,* by Patricia Moore

Introductions:

I. Dr. Bruce Lipton: an American developmental biologist notable for his views on epigenetics. Epigenetics is an emerging field of science that studies heritable changes caused by the activation and deactivation of genes without any change in the underlying DNA sequence of the organism. Revolutionary research has uncovered the missing connections between biology, psychology and spirituality.

II. Dr. Joe Dispenza: Doctor Chiropractor, biochemist, neuroscientist. Reconditioning the Body to a New Mind, Tuning in to New Potentials, Changing Beliefs and Perceptions.

III. Gregg Braden: Gregg is a scientist, geologist, and a leading researcher on human consciousness. He is a NY Times bestselling author and discusses why now is the time to forward to a better future, based on scientific research and ancient wisdom texts.

Inspirations:

I. Rumi, a 13th-century Persian poet, Hanafi faqih, Islamic scholar, Maturidi theologian, and Sufi mystic.

The Art of Living Without Walls: Haute Couture Architecture